To Danil

wishing you lots of

happy fishing days

with love

Vikki   Jan 14th 2014

FISHING

COARSE, GAME AND SEA

FISHING

COARSE, GAME AND SEA

Bruce Vaughan

Abbeydale Press

This edition is published by Abbeydale Press, an imprint of Anness Publishing Ltd, Hermes House, 88–89 Blackfriars Road, London SE1 8HA; tel. 020 7401 2077; fax 020 7633 9499

www.annesspublishing.com

Anness Publishing has a new picture agency outlet for images for publishing, promotions or advertising. Please visit our website www.practicalpictures.com for more information.

© Anness Publishing Ltd 2010

Produced for Anness Publishing Ltd by: Editorial Developments, Edgmond, Shropshire, England Design by: Dave Allen Design

Printed in China

ETHICAL TRADING POLICY
Because of our ongoing ecological investment programme, you, as our customer, can have the pleasure and reassurance of knowing that a tree is being cultivated on your behalf to naturally replace the materials used to make the book you are holding. For further information about this scheme, go to www.annesspublishing.com/trees

Desk Editor: Barbara Toft
Index: Marie Lorimer Indexing Services

PUBLISHER'S NOTE
Although the advice and information in this book are believed to be accurate and true at the time of going to press, neither the authors nor the publisher can accept any legal responsibility or liability for any errors or omissions that may be made nor for any inaccuracies nor for any loss, harm or injury that comes about from following instructions or advice in this book. Codes of Conduct apply to angling practice, and many fisheries have their own sets of rules for use when fishing their waters. The advice and information in this book should in no way replace these regulations.

All measurements in the text are provided according to the imperial system. A metric conversion chart can be found on page 256.

CONTENTS

FOREWORD

There can be few anglers around, whatever their chosen branch of the sport, who will not be inspired or informed by this lavishly illustrated book from the pen of author and life-long angler Bruce Vaughan. Over 200 colour pictures illustrate the informative and accessible text, offering in-depth advice on the three disciplines of coarse, sea and game fishing around the British Isles. There is also a section, which I have had the pleasure to contribute, covering the escalating interest in fishing overseas for the more unusual or monstrous fish to be had in both temperate and far-flung tropical destinations.

So whether you love using a fixed spool reel and Avon rod combo; creeping along on all fours beside an overgrown river while freelining a fat slug for chub; casting artificial lures to pike or pollack with a multiplier outfit; roll-casting a fly to trout and salmon; working a heavy pirk deep down over a wartime wreck off the south coast; or drifting over sandbanks using sand eel bait for bass, turbot or plaice, this volume allows you either to simply browse for a short time through evocatively illustrated pages, or to read extensively through informative text written by experienced enthusiasts, covering baits, tackle and technique. Either way, you'll have trouble putting it down.

John Wilson

Introduction by the author, Bruce Vaughan

T he sport of fishing is one of Britain's most popular pastimes, and offers anybody who wants to try it a constant source of excitement, stimulation and enjoyment.

Divided into three main sections, *Fishing* provides an in-depth guide to all aspects of game, coarse and sea angling. It is lavishly illustrated in full colour, offering sound information on fish identification and location as well as the tackle, tactics and baits required to catch them. In addition, numerous practical tips are provided throughout the book to help you catch all kinds of fish in a variety of situations.

Recognising that many anglers now take or aspire to taking regular fishing holidays abroad, *Fishing* also features a small but detailed section devoted to the sport overseas. Species, tackle and tactics are comprehensively covered, plus advice on how to reach venues as diverse as Lake Nasser and the mighty Zambezi River.

Throughout its informative pages, *Fishing* offers a wealth of practical advice that will prove to be of immense value to any newcomer to the wonderful sport of angling, while also providing some well-tested tips and advice for the seasoned angler.

COARSE FISHING

Coarse fishing offers incredible variety in the number of different species that can be targeted, the diverse environments in which they live, the many and varied methods by which they can be caught and the huge range of tackle and baits that can be used to catch them.

For the past decade or so most coarse species have been growing noticeably larger. This phenomenon is due to a combination of factors that include milder winters and the high nutritional value of many of the baits being used. However, the upshot of it is that there has never been a better time to catch a fish of

BELOW *The development of lightweight materials has seen an increased use of long poles on stillwater and river fisheries alike.*

specimen size, and at least one British record is now being broken each year.

Another exciting prospect for coarse anglers is that every year more and more waters are becoming available to them. Some are newly created stillwater fisheries that frequently boast a full range of on-site facilities including accommodation, secure parking, all-weather fishing pegs, toilets, a bait and tackle shop, café and bar! Many of these fisheries are heavily stocked with carp, ensuring frantic sport, while others offer fishing for a mixture of species, sometimes segregated in a series of pools.

The decline in salmon stocks has also seen many rivers once strictly preserved for game angling opening their doors to coarse anglers – some for the winter months only, when the salmon season is closed, but others for the entire river coarse fishing season (June 16th–March 14th). Some beautiful stretches of the River Wye on the Welsh border, in particular, have now become accessible to coarse fishermen.

Numerous public water supply reservoirs around the country, which were once run as fly-only trout fisheries, now welcome coarse anglers, seeing them as a valuable additional source of revenue. Fishing for predators is primarily from boats, and recent seasons have seen some huge pike and zander landed, with some being taken on flies as well as lures and deadbaits.

This combination of increased access, ever more sophisticated tackle and bait, and fish that are growing bigger means that there has never been a better time to go coarse fishing!

MAIN PICTURE
With no closed season on stillwaters, many coarse fisheries offer year-round sport and a host of facilities for visiting anglers.

LEFT In recent years the carp has supplanted the roach as Britain's most sought-after coarse fish species.

Coarse Species

Barbel
Barbus barbus

IDENTIFICATION

Barbel enjoy a reputation as one of the hardest-fighting species found in UK waters. Irrespective of size, they fight incredibly hard using both speed and power to the last.

In profile, barbel resemble elongated carp – a streamlined shape that enables them to hold bottom comfortably in rapid flows. Like carp, barbel possess two pairs of sensitive barbels (like feelers) above and below their underslung mouth, which assist them in searching out food. The barbel's tough rubbery lips are perfectly designed for

BELOW High summer on a barbel river full of character and interesting fishing spots where the river bottom drops steeply – a known spot to catch barbel.

rooting around on the river bottom among sharp stones and gravel. Barbel can vary in colour from golden-brown to green-brown or even grey-brown.

LOCATION

Barbel were originally restricted to the east-flowing rivers of England such as the Thames and its tributaries, the Great Ouse and rivers in Yorkshire. Over the years, however, barbel have been introduced – both legally and illegally – into many other English and Welsh rivers. Barbel have also been stocked in some

BAITS

- ▶ Hemp and tares
- ▶ Maggots and casters
- ▶ Sweetcorn
- ▶ Processed meats
- ▶ Worms
- ▶ Cheese
- ▶ Boilies
- ▶ Pellets (esp. halibut)

stillwaters, and although they appear to cope, the action has not been without controversy.

FEEDING

The position of the mouth betrays the barbel as primarily a bottom feeder, although they will also rise in the water to take food items. Barbel feed naturally on all manner of aquatic creatures such as shrimps and snails and will also include small fish in their diet.

Although barbel will feed all year round – and particularly at night – they are less likely to feed when the water temperature falls below 5°C, particularly if it is a rapid fall. During winter floods, warm and coloured water fills the river, triggering aggressive feeding in barbel.

HABITAT

Barbel are primarily lovers of fast, clean and well-oxygenated water, though they will live quite happily in slower flows. Barbel like to lie under the cover of long strands of ranunculus (streamer weed), where they can pick off any food items washed downstream. They are also to be found under overhanging trees (often among the roots), in depressions in the riverbed, in drop-offs where the bed falls sharply away from shallow water, and in weirpools. Where weirs have been undercut by years of erosion caused by the river's flow, barbel can be found right under the sill. Barbel are attracted to these snags, and head straight for them when hooked.

WEIGHT

In recent years barbel have been growing significantly larger, and the British rod-caught record now stands at 21lb 1oz. The majority of barbel caught weigh between 3lb and 8lb and any fish over 10lb can be considered to be of specimen size.

ABOVE A splendid brace of barbel. Retain barbel for a short time only in a net or tube positioned in well-oxygenated running water.

FISH'N'TIPS

▶ *During big floods barbel will often lie very close to the bank in pockets of slower water.*

Bream
Abramis brama

IDENTIFICATION

BELOW Bream fishing on a large Irish lake. Prebaiting an area for several days prior to fishing is the accepted method for ensuring big bags of bream.

Two species of bream occur in UK fresh water: the common or bronze bream and the far less common silver bream (*Blicca bjoerkna*). The only time confusion between the species could arise is when bronze bream are small, as then they are also silvery in colour. However, silver bream occur in so few known waters that any that are caught can be assumed to be the common bream.

Bream are a deep-bodied and slim species well covered in slime and known as skimmers or tin plates when small. Once the fish is about 3lb in weight, the back becomes progressively humped and colour changes to bronze or brown, though in some waters bream can show a dark grey or almost black colouring. The bream's mouth is that of a bottom feeder, being underslung. Bream live in shoals, which can sometimes be huge, numbering hundreds of individual fish.

BAITS

▶ **Maggots and casters**
▶ **Bread – paste and flake**
▶ **Lobworms and brandlings**
▶ **Pellets and boilies**

LEFT Bream live in large shoals: a competition angler brings a haul of deep-bodied bronze bream ashore for weighing.

LOCATION

Bronze bream are widespread in the UK and Ireland. Although established in several chalkstreams, including the rivers Test and Avon in Hampshire, they are most common in stillwaters such as the Norfolk Broads, the meres of Shropshire and Cheshire, old estate lakes, reservoirs and gravel pits. They are also regularly to be found in slow-flowing rivers and drains like the Thames, Great Ouse and other rivers in East Anglia, and in the waters of the Somerset levels. In Ireland, the River Shannon in particular is famed for its bream fishing.

FEEDING

Bream are natural feeders on a range of insect larvae (particularly bloodworms), worms and snails. Stillwater bream, especially bigger specimens, will often feed exclusively at night, while even on rivers dawn and dusk are reliably the most productive times for feeding. However, bream will feed in the day, particularly when

there is total cloud cover and on waters that are deep and/or carrying some colour.

HABITAT

Bream are very much a nomadic species, and they need to be, as large shoals will quickly exhaust any source of food discovered. In some waters regular patrol routes become established, and often, when feeding is about to take place, bream will begin rolling and displaying at the surface. When they do get their heads down and start to feed, the bottom quickly becomes stirred up, noticeably colouring the water.

WEIGHT

Bream introduced to gravel pits often flourish, and most double-figure fish reported come from such fisheries. While the average size of bream caught overall is between 2 and 3lb, in gravel pits it is far higher. A 10lb fish is a specimen, but the current British record for a bream is now very close to 20lb at 19lb 10oz.

FISH'N'TIPS

▶ *The watchful angler will look for bream rolling prior to feeding, and for coloured water, where bream will already have started feeding.*

Carp
Cyprinus carpio

BELOW A carp angler battles to keep a good fish out of marginal weeds by applying sidestrain with the rod and tightening the reel's clutch to maximum.

BAITS

▶ **Maggots and casters**
▶ **Bread – paste, crust and flake**
▶ **Boilies and pellets**
▶ **Hemp and tares**
▶ **Sweetcorn**
▶ **Processed meats**
▶ **Nuts**
▶ **Seeds and beans**

IDENTIFICATION

The original strain of carp, known as a wildie, is long, slim, fully scaled and golden brown in colour. The collective term used for the three main varieties of carp that are descended from this original strain is king carp. They were developed through selective breeding many years ago by European fish farmers, who wanted fast-growing fish that could be harvested quickly for the table (many people in Europe eat carp). The trio of king carp varieties comprises common carp, mirror carp and leather carp.

All king carp are much deeper and broader than wild carp, with the potential in rich waters to grow to 50lb or more. Wild carp weighing more than 10lb, on the other hand, are rare – as true wild carp of any weight are,

due to their readiness to breed with king carp, producing hybrid offspring.

Common carp are similar to wildies in being fully scaled. Mirror carp possess a random scattering of large scales across smooth-skinned flanks. Occasionally, fully scaled mirror carp occur with their bodies covered in an array of different-sized scales. Leather carp are virtually devoid of scales, instead sporting thick leathery bodies.

Coloration in king carp varies widely and includes dull brown, golden-brown, yellow, blue-grey, and sometimes dark ruby red. The fins are usually brown or grey-brown, occasionally with orange in the lower fins.

There are two pairs of sensitive barbels above and below the corners of the mouth, which assist the carp in seeking food.

LOCATION

Carp have become the most popular and sought-after species in the UK in the past 30 years or so, and are now to be found in every conceivable type of water. Gravel pits around the country were the first beneficiaries of carp introductions, while over the past two decades many man-made pools have been developed, most stocked with large numbers of carp. Such waters have proven highly popular with pleasure and competition anglers alike, due to the relative ease with which fish can be caught and the huge catches that can be made.

Traditionally a species found in stillwaters, carp have now colonised many canals and river systems as a result of floods, and they have thrived – not least in the chalkstreams formerly preserved for salmon and trout fishing in southern England!

LEFT A typical mirror carp showing its large, scattered scale pattern. Occasionally, fully scaled mirror carp occur that have flanks covered in different-sized scales.

LEFT On leather carp, scales are either totally absent or very small in number. Their bodies are tough and smooth-textured, giving them their name.

FEEDING

Carp feed naturally on all manner of bottom-dwelling creatures including prodigious amounts of midge larvae (bloodworms), shrimps and snails. They also eat some aquatic weeds, and in warmer weather will rise to the surface to take hatching aquatic and windblown terrestrial insects.

HABITAT

In the absence of any bankside disturbance, carp like to take up residence in the margins of mature stillwaters. Here they can enjoy cover, lying under overhanging trees and bushes, near lily pads, weedbeds, undercut banks and close to snags. They love to work along open reed beds close to the bank in search of food, and the quiet angler will be alerted to their presence by seeing the reed stems banging and shaking as the carp progress through them. Carp will also seek out bloodworm beds, and give away their presence when feeding on them by colouring the water and sending streams of bubbles up to the surface.

In large gravel-pit fisheries carp will be attracted to these features if they occur there as well as to gravel bars and offshore islands, around both of which food tends to collect. On big waters, carp are very influenced by the wind. Should a good breeze spring up or the wind change direction, carp will quickly make their way to the downwind shore – often very close in – in search of food.

Carp in rivers can be very nomadic but normally keep to the slacker water found at the margins – on the inside of bends or below lock gates, for example – and seek out similar bankside cover to that found in stillwaters.

WEIGHT

Not only have carp numbers increased dramatically over the decades but their weights have risen also. Whereas once, a 20lb carp was considered a catch of a lifetime, now they are commonplace. A more realistic definition of a specimen carp today would be 30lb or perhaps even 40lb. The current British record carp weighed 65lb 14oz.

European Catfish or Wels
Siluris glanis

BAITS

- ► Live and dead fish
- ► Worms
- ► Luncheon meat
- ► Fish-based pellets and boilies

IDENTIFICATION

It is impossible to mistake the wels for any other species. Specimens weighing over 100lb are now being caught and, with the potential for them to grow larger still, they are undoubtedly the largest predatory fish swimming in UK waters.

The fleshy and powerful body is long and tapers from a large flat head down to a small tail. The dorsal fin is small while the anal fin is very long, like that of an eel. Body colouring is mottled and can be brown-grey or olive, or a combination of colours (depending on environment) on the flanks, with a white belly below. The catfish's eyes are tiny but the mouth is huge and contains two patches of small teeth – one on the top and one on the bottom jaw – that feel rough to the touch. Wels catfish possess six barbels positioned at the side of the mouth and under the chin to assist them in locating prey.

LOCATION

The first major introduction of catfish into the UK occurred at the end of the nineteenth century, when the Duke of Bedford stocked the lakes on his estate at Woburn Abbey with 70 small specimens. Over time, catfish were taken from there to several stillwaters around

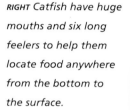

RIGHT Catfish have huge mouths and six long feelers to help them locate food anywhere from the bottom to the surface.

BELOW Catfish will thrive in any water containing sizeable populations of small fish. They are particularly partial to the bottom-dwelling tench.

LEFT *Once localised, catfish are now present in over 100 UK fisheries through legal and illegal introductions. On the Continent, catfish weighing over 500lb have also been caught!*

Leighton Buzzard, and also to Claydon Lakes in Buckinghamshire. Until a few decades ago, these waters were the only fisheries known to contain catfish, apart from only a handful of others.

Now the situation has totally changed, with catfish widespread in over 100 waters as a result of both legal and illegal introductions, some of the latter being into rivers including the Thames and Great Ouse.

FEEDING

Catfish will feed on a variety of items, including living and dead fish, freshwater mussels, frogs and even occasionally waterfowl and swimming rodents. Tench are considered to be a favoured food of catfish.

It has become increasingly apparent in recent years that catfish will not only search for food on the bottom but readily move up in the water column – including right at the surface – to take food.

HABITAT

Any water that offers ample feeding will suit catfish. They appreciate areas of deeper water, weedbeds or snags in which to lie up during daylight hours before venturing into more open water at dusk to feed. They will feed during the day in dull, overcast conditions but are not active in bright sunshine. Under cover of darkness they will move right into the margins and very shallow water in search of food.

WEIGHT

On the Continent, catfish over 500lb have been caught, so nobody really knows the maximum potential in the UK. Currently most catfish caught in UK waters weigh below 20lb, and a 30lb-plus fish is considered a specimen. There is currently no British record, since it is impossible to differentiate between indigenous catfish and huge fish that have been illegally imported.

FISH'N'TIPS

▶ *Catfish are most active on moonless, humid nights following hot summer days.*

Chub
Leuciscus cephalus

BELOW Casting natural baits, such as large slugs and lobworms, to visible chub is an exciting summer technique. Tread quietly and use bankside vegetation for cover.

BAITS

- ▶ **Live fish**
- ▶ **Dead fish**
- ▶ **Bread – crust, flake and paste**
- ▶ **Maggots and casters**
- ▶ **Crayfish and lampreys**
- ▶ **Wasp nests**
- ▶ **Hemp and tares**
- ▶ **Slugs and lobworms**
- ▶ **Cheese**
- ▶ **Cheese paste**
- ▶ **Caddis grubs (sedge larvae)**
- ▶ **Boilies and pellets**
- ▶ **Fruits and berries**
- ▶ **Sweetcorn**
- ▶ **Cooked peeled prawns**
- ▶ **Processed meats**

IDENTIFICATION

During the summer chub are normally slim and richly coloured with dark, brassy gold flanks. In the winter their big scales, though still black trimmed, turn to silver. The chub's dorsal and tail fin are coloured blue-black, while its lower fins range from a delicate coral pink to orange. Chub living in permanently coloured water exhibit paler colouring, as do all chub after prolonged floods.

Small chub can be mistaken for big dace although the chub's blunt head, huge mouth and white lips are obvious differences. Another distinguishing feature is that the chub's dorsal and anal fin edges curve out (convex) while on a dace they curve in (concave). At first glance chub and grass carp might look similar, but there are many differences – for one thing, chub don't grow to 40lb!

LOCATION

Chub are widespread throughout most of the rivers of England, southern Scotland and east Wales. Although not indigenous to Ireland, chub are now present in the River Inny near Mullingar after being illegally stocked some years ago. Chub can be found in the smallest stream to the largest river and are as at home in the upper rocky reaches of game rivers,

such as the Wye and Severn, as they are in the slower-flowing rivers of the Midlands (Thames/Ouse) and the lush chalkstreams (Test/Kennet) of southern England. Chub are now commonly found in stillwaters as well – particularly in gravel pits close to river systems.

FEEDING

Chub are omnivorous, enjoying a diet that includes both living and dead fish, fruits (plums, cherries) and berries (elderberries, blackberries), worms, slugs, beetles, hatching aquatic flies (mayfly) and windblown terrestrial flies (crane fly), shrimps and various types of weed.

HABITAT

Chub like living by and under cover, particularly in the form of overhanging trees and bushes. In the summer these provide shade, security (snaggy root systems) and food (a variety of creatures fall from the branches and leaves). In autumn and winter, trailing branches from the bushes and trees catch vegetation floating downstream. This builds up in time to form a solid raft or roof over the chub's head – again offering the fish security.

Chub are also attracted to undercut banks and beneath eroded weir sills, deep water in weirpools, the areas of slack water among and behind mid-river weedbeds (e.g. bulrushes) and under mats of floating marginal weeds such as watercress.

In the winter, chub look for comfortable flows, and in times of high water they will occupy the "crease" (junction) that occurs between the main flow of the river and slacker water close in.

Stillwater chub can be largely nomadic and are very difficult to locate. In summer, they may be visible basking at the surface. If not, look for features that may attract chub to a specific area, like overhanging or sunken trees and bushes, inflowing streams or evidence of shoals of fry or small fish.

WEIGHT

Chub are growing bigger, with many rivers now producing numerous chub in the 5 to 6lb bracket, while reports of chub caught weighing over 7lb are a regular occurrence. The British record now stands at 9lb 5oz – caught from still water.

ABOVE Constantly feeding a swim with baits such as maggots, hemp and casters will often result in chub losing their natural caution, enabling large numbers to be caught.

FISH'N'TIPS

▶ *Floating diving plugs are often highly effective, both for river and stillwater chub, in the half-light of early morning during summer.*

BAITS

- ▶ Maggots and casters
- ▶ Hemp and tares
- ▶ Worms
- ▶ Bread – paste and flake

Dace
Leuciscus leuciscus

BELOW Trotting for dace on a crisp winter's day with an Avon rod and centrepin reel. Centrepins provide superior float control when compared with fixed-spool reels.

IDENTIFICATION

Although similar in appearance to chub, dace are a slimmer, altogether more delicate species that rarely grow larger than 1lb (see "Chub" for further differences).

Whereas the dace's flanks are always silvery, its fin coloration can vary widely. In the clearwater chalkstreams of southern England, which offer rich feeding, the fins of the dace can often be a deep and rich pink or orange in colour, while on rivers with less water clarity the fins are more often a translucent white.

During late winter the sexes separate prior to spawning, and at this time the males lose most of their protective slime and feel rough and dry to the touch.

LOCATION

While dace occasionally occur in lakes, their natural home is flowing water. They thrive in the upper reaches of streams and rivers where currents are strong and the water quality high. Conversely, they sometimes occur in the very lowest parts of a river and even in tidal reaches, and here they can be found in huge numbers, though individuals are small.

Dace can be found throughout the waterways of England and Wales, and

although rare in Scotland, they are increasing their range in Ireland.

FEEDING

Dace will take food from the surface to the bottom of the water column, and generally need little encouragement to feed at any time of the year. Constantly loose-feeding a swim with free offerings while fishing can induce a feeding frenzy in a shoal of dace.

BELOW A big dace from Berkshire's River Kennet. The chalkstreams of southern England produce the most vividly coloured dace, often to specimen size.

HABITAT

Dace are normally to be found in the main flow of the river, where they are ready to intercept any food item that might be brought their way by the current. Larger specimens will sometimes seek out slower, deeper water on the edge of the flow, probably to conserve energy. Long glides containing beds of ranunculus (streamer weed) are popular with dace, providing them with protection, cover and a source of food. The tail end of weirpools, where the water becomes shallow and speeds up, is also often frequented by dace.

WEIGHT

Dace weighing more than 1lb are exceedingly rare and any fish over 12oz can be considered a specimen. The current British record dace weighed a mighty 1lb 5oz 2dr.

ABOVE A plump female dace in prime condition. Dace are at their heaviest in late February to early March, just prior to spawning.

FISH'N'TIPS

▶ *Strong-smelling cheese paste, as used for chub, can also attract big dace during periods of high, coloured water.*

Eel
Anguilla anguilla

BAITS

- ▶ Live fish
- ▶ Dead fish
- ▶ Lobworms
- ▶ Maggots
- ▶ Fish-based boilies and pellets

IDENTIFICATION

The European freshwater eel resembles a snake, with its long sinuous body and small head. The body is fleshy and muscular and covered in thick slime – all of which makes it difficult to keep hold of. The eel's back is dark and is most commonly a mixture of brown and yellow, and the belly is creamy white. Both the dorsal and anal fins are very long and meet at the tail.

LOCATION

The European eel breeds in the Sargasso Sea, an area of the Atlantic Ocean close to the equator. The larvae of the eels travel with the Gulf Stream across the ocean, and after one to three years, their leptocephali reach a size of 3–3$^1/_2$ inches by the time they reach the coasts of Europe. Because their tiny bodies are now transparent, they are commonly known as glass eels. On reaching the coastal areas they migrate up rivers and streams, overcoming all sorts of natural challenges and finally reaching even the smallest of creeks. They can

BELOW Eels can be safely retained in a carp sack until daylight, when they can be photographed.

move themselves over wet grass and dig through wet sand so they can reach upstream headwaters and ponds. In freshwater they develop pigmentation, turn into elvers (young eels) and feed on creatures such as small crustaceans, worms and insects.

As a result, eels can be found in virtually every type of water, though bigger specimens are generally found in stillwaters – particularly in weedy, snaggy fisheries containing plenty of small prey fish. By the time they reach 10–14 years old, they will have grown to a length of 2–2$^1/_2$ feet.

When mature, eels will at some stage feel the urge to spawn – though maturity can be at any age from 6 to 20 years. They will then make their way back to the sea for the long journey south to the Sargasso Sea.

In recent years, the number of elvers arriving at European waters has dropped dramatically – some say by as much as 90 per cent. It is believed that overfishing and changes to the Gulf Stream are two major causes of the dramatic decline.

LEFT Specimen eels can be very old so treat them with care. An eel weighing nearly 6¹/₂lb was found to be almost 70 years old.

FEEDING

The natural diet of eels includes live and dead fish, frogs, coarse fish spawn and crustaceans such as crayfish. They are most active at night, particularly during periods of hot and humid weather. The eel is most definitely a fish of the summer months. Although primarily a bottom feeder, it will search for food at all depths in the water column, including taking food right at the surface.

HABITAT

Eels like to be in areas with cover, especially during the day, when they tend to shun the light. Dense weedbeds and snags in particular will attract them. On canals they are often found around lock structures and under bridges. Underwater tree root systems and undercut banks – including crumbling brickwork – will also find favour with eels.

Sometimes, in clearwater lakes and rivers, just the heads of eels can be seen poking out of the bed. These eels have buried their bodies in the soft sand or silt at the bottom for safety reasons, and emerge to feed as the security of dusk arrives.

ABOVE The British record eel caught from a lake near Ringwood in Hampshire. A truly exceptional fish, it beat the previous record by nearly 3lb and may never be bettered.

WEIGHT

Big eels are not only rare, but can also be very old: one eel weighing nearly 6¹/₂lb was found to be almost 70 years old! So, treat any big eel captured with great care. A 3lb eel is a respectable size, while anything over 5lb is a specimen. The current British record catch is truly exceptional at 11lb 2oz.

Perch
Perca fluviatilis

IDENTIFICATION

With its boldly striped flanks, orangey-red fins and spiked front dorsal fin and gill covers, the perch could not be confused with any other UK species. The black-barred olive-brown flanks offer perch excellent camouflage when hunting their prey, while their large eyes enable them to hunt effectively when light levels are low early and late in the day.

LOCATION

After disappearing from many fisheries during the 1970s and 1980s through endemic disease, perch have made a dramatic comeback over the past decade and are now widespread again. They can be found in every type of watercourse throughout the British Isles.

FEEDING

Small fish make up a large part of a perch's diet, particularly during the summer. Perch have also been known to eat their own kind. Lobworms make up another part, while in recent years the American signal crayfish has become a significant part of the perch's diet, as this fast-growing and aggressive crustacean

LEFT The perch's green, black-striped body is perfect camouflage when lying alongside reed beds.
BELOW Perch feed more boldly during the day when the water is coloured.

ABOVE A splendid quartet of perch taken on float-fished lobworm. Regular feeding with chopped worms is essential to hold perch in a swim.

has rapidly spread to numerous fisheries. In many waters this introduced crayfish has reached plague proportions, and this is probably the main reason why perch have become so big.

HABITAT

Perch are often the first species to arrive in a new body of water such as a recently flooded gravel pit – probably because perch eggs are extremely sticky and adhere to the legs and feet of waterfowl browsing for food in marginal weed where perch eggs are laid. Perch, in common with other predators, like to operate from cover, and in rivers they lie up next to reed and rush beds and under overhanging trees – particularly those with weed rafts. Perch are also attracted to lock cuttings, half-submerged fallen trees, the slacker water to the side of weir sills and even under moored boats – anywhere, in fact, where small fish and fry congregate.

In lakes perch will group up under lily pads or descend into deeper water for cover, but then they will move into the shallows to attack fry shoals – most frequently at dawn but also at dusk. During the winter, perch will migrate to the deeper parts of a lake and feed on invertebrates, crustaceans and any other fish species encountered there.

ABOVE A specimen perch from the Great Ouse near Buckingham.

WEIGHT

Any perch weighing over 3lb can be considered a specimen, though in an increasing number of waters a 4lb fish is a distinct possibility. The British record perch weighed 5lb 15oz.

FISH'N'TIPS

▶ *Fish as close to weedbeds as possible – particularly during the day when light values are higher.*

Pike

Esox lucius

BAITS

- ▶ Live fish
- ▶ Dead fish
- ▶ Artificial lures – plugs, spoons and spinners

BELOW A big pike from the Norfolk Broads – a venue renowned for the quality of its winter pike fishing, and where going afloat offers the best chance of success.

IDENTIFICATION

Although catfish grow larger, pike are the biggest predatory species found naturally in UK waters. Pike are long and slim in profile and are superbly camouflaged for ambushing their prey.

Their flanks can be a variable mix of greens, browns, grey and yellow, depending on the environment, but they are always liberally scattered with yellow-white spots. Their tails are powerful and designed for short bursts of speed, while their mouths are

ABOVE A large pike lies beaten and ready for netting. The successful method: a dead roach fished below a sliding float setup.

Larger and older fish will tend to turn to scavenging for food, preferring to eat dead fish than expend valuable energy chasing prey.

HABITAT

Pike – especially big pike – thrive on undisturbed waters, so the angler discovering an area containing pike is generally advised to keep it confidential.

Pike remain close to cover when ambushing and hunting in order to stay well camouflaged from their prey. Weedbeds, rafts of weed caught by trailing tree branches, the root systems of trees and depressions in the lake or river bed all allow pike to remain unobtrusive. Even abandoned vehicles in gravel pits will be used by pike as ambush points!

FISH'N'TIPS

▶ *Pike can be attracted into a new swim by prebaiting with chopped or whole small fish.*

BELOW Although pike look fearsome, with big mouths full of sharp teeth, they are in fact delicate creatures that need to be handled with care during unhooking.

ABOVE Pike can sometimes become preoccupied with a particular size of prey. This near-20lb pike was seen feeding on fry and quickly fell for a small Mepp spinner.

filled with hundreds of sharp teeth, many sloping backwards to prevent any grabbed prey from escaping.

LOCATION

Pike are to be found throughout the British Isles – in streams, rivers and canals and in waters ranging from the smallest village pond to the huge lakes of Scotland and Ireland that extend to many thousands of acres.

FEEDING

Pike will eat a wide variety of items as well as fish. Smaller pike will eat worms and slugs while all sizes of pike will take frogs, crayfish, waterfowl (particularly young ones) and swimming rodents such as rats and voles.

Pike are one of the few species that you can fish for with bait that is their natural food – i.e. fish.

WEIGHT

Pike have not grown in size as a species in the way others have in recent years. A 20lb pike is still recognised as the benchmark of a specimen. Some 30-pounders are caught each year and are often from trout reservoirs, but any pike over 40lb is extremely rare. The British record stands at 46lb 13oz and was taken from a trout fishery.

Roach
Rutilus rutilus

BAITS

- ▶ Hemp and tares
- ▶ Bread – crust, flake and paste
- ▶ Cheese
- ▶ Maggots and casters
- ▶ Sweetcorn
- ▶ Wheat and barley
- ▶ Pellets and boilies
- ▶ Worms

IDENTIFICATION

Until the explosive growth in carp fishing, roach were always the most sought-after coarse species. In summer their silvery scaled bodies often exhibit a golden tinge, which in winter changes to a steely blue. Fin colour varies from a pale yellow to deep orange, with roach from waters with high clarity – chalkstreams and gravel pits – showing the strongest coloration.

LOCATION

Roach are widely distributed throughout the UK and Ireland and can be found in every kind of water from streams and rivers to canals, sand and gravel pits, lakes, reservoirs and small ponds. Very big roach are now being caught in an increasing number of carp fisheries, where they are feeding on the highly nutritional baits intended for the carp!

BELOW When roach fishing in winter, present the bait on the crease between fast and slow water; it is there that roach hold position to intercept any food items washed downstream.

LEFT Trotting thumbnail-sized pieces of breadflake is an invaluable method for landing winter roach, as long as you regularly feed them with liquidised or mashed bread.

BELOW A trio of roach taken by float fishing with a light match rod and centrepin reel. Roach feed most confidently at dawn and dusk and on a rising river.

FEEDING

Roach feed at all levels in the water column on foods such as insect larvae (bloodworms), snails, shrimps and some weeds. They are at their most active in low-light conditions, and in rivers they begin to feed aggressively as water levels rise and colour up after heavy rainfall.

HABITAT

On rivers, roach like comfortable water off the main flow. They particularly like cover in the form of overhanging trees, especially where rafts of weed have built up on trailing branches, or close beside and behind beds of rush and ranunculus (streamer weed). On large stillwaters roach can be nomadic, seeking out gravel bars and currents caused by the wind, inflowing streams or springs.

Unusually for fish of slower-flowing water, roach will often be seen rolling right out in the fastest water during a flood. In fact, roach will frequently show at the surface in the early morning and late evening, and this act of "priming" is of great assistance to the angler in locating a shoal.

WEIGHT

Whereas many species have shown significant weight gain in recent times, this is not the case where roach are concerned, bar in a few exceptional stillwater fisheries. The target specimen weight for roach is still 2lb, though a 2lb roach from a river is a much tougher proposition than it used to be. The British record now stands at 4lb 4oz – a truly exceptional fish.

FISH'N'TIPS

▶ *Whole lobworms can be invaluable for big roach when the river is high and coloured.*

Rudd
Scardinius erythrophtalmus

BAITS

- Bread – floating crust and flake
- Maggots
- Casters – particularly floating
- Sweetcorn

IDENTIFICATION

Rudd are similar in shape to roach, but have deeper bellies and are far more richly coloured. The rudd's flanks are covered in large golden-yellow scales, while their fins can vary from bright orange through to a beautiful deep crimson. The mouth of the rudd is upturned with its prominent lower jaw showing its preference for feeding at the surface.

LOCATION

Rudd have become increasingly rare over recent decades through loss of habitat and the fact that they frequently crossbreed with roach and bream to produce hybrids. They do occur in some gravel pits – particularly in the southern half of England – where they often grow to specimen size.

Neglected farm ponds and old estate lakes will also sometimes be found to contain rudd, but in such waters they often overbreed – resulting in fisheries filled with myriad

BELOW A small piece of breadflake cast gently ahead of a group of cruising rudd will often be engulfed as it sinks.

stunted, half-starved fish that are of not much interest to anglers.

Even in Ireland, once a stronghold of true rudd, the rapid spread of roach through the country's lake and river systems has sadly resulted in them becoming much less common.

FEEDING

Although nature designed rudd for surface feeding, they will also take food at midwater and at the bottom. Slow-sinking baits fished on long hooklengths can be highly effective, as can buoyant baits presented just off bottom. Rudd feed naturally on various aquatic creatures at every depth including the bed, as well as taking hatching and windblown terrestrial insects at the surface.

HABITAT

On larger waters, rudd can be very nomadic, staying well out from the bank, and are constantly on the move in search of food.

LEFT With their golden-scaled flanks and scarlet fins, rudd are one of our most beautiful coarse fish. The upturned mouth shows it is primarily a surface feeder.

FISH'N'TIPS

▶ *Fish with the wind behind you in order to drift floating hookbaits and fish-attracting free offerings well out from the bank.*

BELOW A specimen rudd taken from shallow water on casters fished under a waggler float. Big rudd live in small shoals and are very nomadic by nature.

In summer, the shoals will cruise along high in the water; their location is given away to the angler when the surface is cut by the backs of the rising fish.

In smaller stillwaters, rudd tend to stay closer to weedbeds and rush beds and only venture out into more open water as the light fades.

Although once thought of as a fish of the summer, rudd can also be caught during the colder months of the year, particularly from deeper gravel pits with bottom-fished baits.

WEIGHT

As with roach, 2lb has long been considered the weight at which a rudd can be regarded as a specimen. The current record of 4lb 10oz is held by two fish and is probably the toughest on the record fish list to surpass.

BAITS

- ▶ Bread – flake and paste
- ▶ Lobworms
- ▶ Sweetcorn
- ▶ Pellets and boilies
- ▶ Maggots and casters
- ▶ Hemp

Tench
Tinca tinca

IDENTIFICATION

With solidly built bodies and large convex-edged fins, tench are quite different from any other fish species. Their bodies are covered in tiny scales coated with thick slime, giving them a fleshy feel when handled. Their colour varies according to the water in which they live, with tench in old estate lakes or ponds usually coloured dark green, sometimes bordering on black. In clearwater gravel pits, the green hue is much less intense and is often more yellow to blend in better with their environment.

All the fins are coloured grey and the tench's eyes are small and bright red. There are also two small barbels at the mouth edge. Male tench grow to only half the size of the females, but have much larger pelvic fins.

BELOW Early morning tench fishing on an old estate lake. In such waters tench will only feed actively from dawn until the sun's rays hit the water.

Although for much of the time tench lead a sedentary life, they are great fighters, showing an impressive combination of strength and speed when hooked.

LOCATION

Until after the Second World War, when gravel-pit fisheries were developed throughout the country, tench were always associated with old farm ponds, monastery pools, estate lakes, canals, drains and a few slow-flowing rivers. Gravel pits, however, have transformed tench fishing, with the species attaining far higher weights in these rich environments than ever before. Tench are found throughout the UK and Ireland.

FISH'N'TIPS

▶ *Thoroughly rake your chosen swim to clear weed and stir up natural food items. Then, bait the area for several days before fishing and you will likely find it full of tench.*

FEEDING

Tench are for the most part bottom feeders and spend their time grubbing around for food items such as insect larvae, shrimps and snails in the silt and mud, sending up sheets of small bubbles as they do so.

On traditional waters, tench feed best around dawn, but this feeding period will normally finish the moment the sun's rays strike the lake's surface. Paradoxically, in gravel pits, tench will be at their most active and feeding hard on days with bright sunshine and high temperatures.

HABITAT

In their traditional haunts tench like to lie close to or even right in weedbeds, and show a particular liking for areas below lily pads. By comparison, in large gravel pits tench spend much of their time on the move in search of food. Early in the summer, they tend to patrol up and down the margins, particularly along the drop-off between deep and shallow water. Although tench do occasionally turn up in the winter, they are primarily a fish of the summer months.

WEIGHT

Tench weights – particularly where gravel-pit fish are concerned – have soared in recent decades, with double-figure fish now regularly reported where once a 5lb fish was a notable capture. Whatever the reasons for this phenomenon, it has totally transformed tench fishing, where the current British record weight is 15lb 3oz 6dr.

ABOVE *The typical pale colouring seen on gravel-pit tench. Pit tench will feed during even bright and sunny days – particularly when it is windy.*

BAITS
▶ Freshwater fish –
dead and alive
▶ Artificial lures –
plugs and
spinners

Zander
Stizostedian lucioperca

IDENTIFICATION

Zander are a predatory species first introduced to England well over 100 years ago. Their body colour graduates from a dark olive-brown back through lighter coloured flanks to a white belly. While slim in shape like a pike, zander share with perch a double dorsal fin, the first of which is spiked, and rough scales coated with little slime.

Zander also possess large, opalescent eyes that glow eerily when lit by a torch beam or camera flash. The mouth is full of small teeth that angle backwards to prevent prey escaping, and additional pairs of long teeth at the front of the mouth are used to stab and hold any fish grabbed.

LOCATION

Zander first found a home in England on the Woburn Abbey estate in Bedfordshire in the late nineteenth century. In time, samples from the lakes there were introduced to other local stillwaters, but it was not until Norfolk's Relief Channel was stocked in the 1960s that the species became more widespread. Today, many fisheries – river, stillwater and canal – in the Midlands and the south of the country contain zander. They are still most widespread in the waterways of eastern England, but are now to be found as far west as the River Severn.

FEEDING

Zander show a marked dislike for bright light and feed most actively when light levels are low at dawn and dusk and into dark. Coloured water also triggers aggressive feeding – particularly during summer and autumn floods. Zander feed in packs of similarly sized fish. They will take freshwater fish prey alive or dead but, unlike pike, show little interest in sea fish baits.

BELOW Zander fishing is popular on the fenland drains of East Anglia, where they have become widespread since their introduction in the late 1960s.

ABOVE A fine brace of winter zander. Zander hunt aggressively at first and last light, and also during the day when the water is coloured after rain.

LEFT An average-sized zander. Zander hunt in packs and prey heavily on small roach and bream. Unlike pike, they will not eat sea deadbaits.

HABITAT

Packs of zander will never be far from the shoals of fish on which they prey, shoals that are attracted to features and structures that afford cover in the water. Such places include lock cuttings, marinas, weedbeds and snags such as fallen trees and tree root systems, and it is here zander are found. In drains and pits, zander will also work close in along the marginal shelf where the bottom drops away into deeper water.

WEIGHT

Although zander are considered to be a fresh-water fish predator, the record zander was taken on a fish-flavoured pellet intended for bream on the lower River Severn! It weighed 21lb 5oz. A 10lb zander is a specimen, with most of those caught weighing between 2lb and 5lb.

FISH'N'TIPS

▶ One of the most effective zander baits is a section of freshwater eel or lamprey.

BAITS

- ▶ Sweetcorn
- ▶ Maggots and casters
- ▶ Breadflake
- ▶ Lobworm

FISH'N'TIPS

▶ *Crucian carp are attracted to silty, weed-lined margins, so adopt a stealthy approach when targeting them.*

Crucian Carp
Carassius carassius

IDENTIFICATION

The huge increase in popularity of carp fishing over recent decades, and the stocking of many fisheries with the species, has caused a severe decline in the population of true crucian carp. This is due to the crucian carp breeding freely with other carp resulting in the species rapidly disappearing from a fishery.

Many carp and crucian carp hybrids – as well as brown goldfish – are mistakenly identified as true crucians. Hybrids, brown goldfish and true crucians have no barbels, whereas carp sport four barbels in pairs above and below the mouth.

Identifying features of a true crucian carp include a very stubby body, rounded tail and a relatively short convex dorsal fin.

LOCATION

BELOW A fine bag of true crucians from a woodland pool.

The only place to be sure of finding true crucian carp are in waters without carp or goldfish in them. Search out neglected waters – particularly old farm ponds or undisturbed pools in woodland settings. Crucians are not present in Scotland or Ireland.

FEEDING

Crucians feed very delicately, and often the only indication that they are present will be the patches of tiny bubbles erupting at the water's surface. These are caused when the fish suck up silt containing food items from the lake bed, then expel all the inedible material. Bait presentation thus needs to be very sensitive to show up the smallest of bites. Crucian carp feed most confidently at dawn and dusk and into dark, and at this time bites ncan be bolder. They are very much a fish of summer and are not usually worth pursuing at any other time of the year.

HABITAT

Crucian carp like to feed over a soft and silty bottom, even if the water is very shallow, particularly where beds of lilies or rushes occur.

WEIGHT

In small stillwaters, crucian carp frequently overbreed, leading to fisheries full of stunted fish that rarely exceed half a pound. The British crucian carp record now stands at 4lb 9oz 9dr, with 2lb being the weight at which a crucian is considered a specimen.

BELOW Crucian carp feed over silty bottoms and give away their presence by small bubbles at the surface.

Grass Carp
Ctenopharynagodon idella

Grass carp originate from China and were first stocked in a small number of English lakes about 20 years ago. They were introduced by several water companies to clear the excessive weed growth that was ruining the lakes. Grass carp cannot breed in the UK so their introduction was not considered a threat. Since then, grass carp have been brought in to more waters in England and Wales, but their distribution is still very limited.

Looking like a cross between a chub and a mullet, grass carp are long and slim, covered in large, black-edged scales. The body is a dark grey-brown on top graduating to yellow-grey flanks. Although great eaters of weed, grass carp will take anglers' baits and are avid surface feeders. They can be caught on bread, maggots, sweetcorn, boilies and pellets.

There is now a British record for the grass carp, which currently stands at 44lb 8oz.

LEFT Unhooking a grass carp tempted by a floating pellet. Although grass carp are primarily weed eaters, they will also take a variety of baits, particularly off the surface.

FISH'N'TIPS

▶ Grass carp are enthusiastic surface feeders.

LEFT A grass carp caught using a controller float to transport a lightweight buoyant bait. Free offerings gain the carp's confidence before the hookbait is cast out.

Bleak, Gudgeon & Minnow
Albernus albernus, Gobio gobio & Phoxinus phoxinus

These three common yet minor species rarely exceed a few ounces in weight. They are shoal species and sometimes occur in large numbers – particularly in the case of bleak. All make excellent baits for predatory species, while minnows in particular can be an extremely effective bait for trout and chub when trotted through stream water in early summer.

IDENTIFICATION

Bleak are a slim, silvery-sided fish with a green back and pale fins. Their eyes are large and the mouth upturned.

Gudgeon are similar in shape to barbel and also have an underslung mouth, though they possess only two mouth barbels. Their bodies are speckled with a blend of blues and browns.

The minnow's coloration consists of a brown back and silver-yellow flanks that are overlaid with green/brown blotches or smudges. Their scales are small, giving the minnow a soft, fleshy feel.

LOCATION

All three species are most commonly found in streams and rivers, although gudgeon and bleak also fare well in stillwaters, especially in gravel pits. Minnows are a great indicator of water quality, being highly intolerant of pollutants.

While minnows are found throughout the UK, bleak and gudgeon are absent from Scotland. Bleak are also present in the River Wye, which borders England and Wales.

FEEDING

The upturned mouth of the bleak shows that it feeds from midwater to the surface, while the underslung mouth of the gudgeon indicates it is a confirmed bottom feeder. With their level lips, minnows will take food anywhere from the top of the water to the river bed.

BAITS

All three species feed avidly on
- Maggots
- Bread
- Small worms

BELOW A silvery-sided bleak with its large eyes and upturned mouth. They were once farmed for their scales, which were used to make artificial pearls.

HABITAT

Gudgeon like clean, sandy and gravelly river beds, whereas bleak thrive in slower-flowing rivers or sections of rivers. Minnows prefer the edges of fast-flowing waters.

WEIGHT

Whereas gudgeon and bleak weighing up to 5oz can be found, minnows are generally lighter, and only weigh up to 2oz.

RIGHT *Gudgeon look similar to barbel, but they have only two barbels at the corners of the mouth instead of four and are much smaller.*

BELOW *Minnows feed at every level in the water column from the surface to the bottom and can occur in very large shoals. They are highly intolerant of pollution.*

FISH'N'TIPS

▶ *All three species make excellent baits for predators like chub, perch and trout.*

Watercraft

'Time spent on reconnaissance is never wasted' is an old military adage that holds just as true for angling. To be able to catch fish it is essential to know where they live and why they choose to live there, something that is best learned by spending time at the waterside.

Many anglers choose swims based on personal comfort – like a short walk from the car – rather than the optimum places in which fish are likely to be found. Anglers who are prepared to invest time and effort in locating their chosen quarry will always gain greater satisfaction and enjoyment, and be more successful.

The river in summer

Generally, rivers will be running lower and with greater clarity during the summer than at any other time of the year, making it an excellent time to gauge the potential of a fishery – particularly one being visited for the first time. Stealthily walking the banks and scanning the water while wearing a pair of polarising sunglasses will reveal many of the species present, and also give an idea of the sizes to which they will grow.

Low, clear water conditions also allow many of the features that attract different species to be seen. Look for sudden drop-offs from shallow to deep water.

In summer, chub will often be spotted quietly cruising shallow areas from which they can rapidly retreat to the safety of nearby deeper water if disturbed. Barbel may also be seen with them on the shallows, but if not visible, could well be holding in the deep water. Dace, grayling and roach are also lovers of gravelly and sandy shallows during summer, and will seek out smooth glides on which to hold station ad feed. All of these species will look for depressions in the riverbed, however small, for a more comfortable lie with the }main flow passing over their heads.

Cover

Most species are attracted to overhanging trees and bushes, particularly where the river deepens and slows. Both the overhead canopy and the snaggy underwater root system offer cover, while a wide variety of creatures (caterpillars, beetles etc) will fall from the branches and leaves into the water. Overhanging elder trees and bramble bushes will also provide a food source as berries fall into the river from late summer.

Other features to look out for include undercut banks and areas of slower, deeper water, which offer cover to bigger chub and an ambush point for species such as pike and perch. Chub and barbel like to position themselves near snags as well as behind beds of bulrushes and under ranunculus (streamer weed), from where they can move into the main flow to intercept food items being carried downstream. Where watercress grows out from the bank, forming rafts of surface vegetation, chub will often be found lying underneath – even when the water is only inches deep.

Perch and pike like to lie in quieter water alongside beds of reeds, marginal cabbages and lily pads, where their superb camouflage renders them invisible to any passing prey.

River bream and tench also generally favour quieter, deeper stretches of river bordered by lily pads, though in summer bream can sometimes be found shoaled up in relatively fast-flowing water.

Fish location on Big Rivers

On some big rivers, fish location can be a much more difficult proposition at all times of the year. Their course is often straight or gently meandering, the depth shows little variation and few features exist on the bank or in the water to offer assistance. On such rivers finding and catching fish is very much a matter of putting in the time and visiting the water as often as possible. Baiting swims on a regular basis can draw fish to them and look for signs of fish rolling – especially roach and bream – at dawn and dusk.

FISH'N'TIPS

▶ *Always wear polarising sunglasses when fish spotting – grey or brown lenses on bright days, yellow lenses on dull days.*

ABOVE During the summer many species can be found holding station over gravelly shallows ready to intercept food items brought their way by the current.

The river in winter

When winter rains arrive, raising water levels and increasing flows, some species like chub and roach will seek out more comfortable water in which to hold up. These deeper, slower-flowing areas are not normally far from the places they inhabit in the warmer months, and are well worth noting during summer when the water is lower and clearer. Other species such as tench, bream, pike and perch will have little need to move having spent much of the summer in slacker parts of the river, which will prove an equally suitable home in winter. During the autumn and into the winter, the branches of bankside trees and bushes that trail in the water, as well as fallen trees lying half-submerged in the river, will catch any leaves and strands of dying weed that drift downstream. Trees out of the main flow will have their branches build up substantial rafts of debris. Underneath them the light levels remain low at all times, and such swims, with their slower flows, are highly attractive to many species including chub, roach, bream, pike and perch.

BELOW Float-fishing for perch on the edge of the current. During winter many species will take up position on the crease that occurs between fast and slow-flowing water.

Slack Water
The blackened stumps of bulrushes that have died back may well still be just visible above the water, but even when they are not, their presence will still be indicated by a broken rippling of the surface. Even in this reduced state these rushbeds still have enough resistance to deflect the river's flow resulting in the water immediately downstream of them being much slacker. These slack areas are great holding places for species such as chub, barbel, pike and perch.

Depressions in the riverbed favoured by species such as roach, chub and barbel during the summer months will continue to be used by them in winter, provided they afford the fish adequate shelter from the full flow of the river. Such depressions are especially likely to be occupied when they occur in an area of river with extensive shallows and few alternative holding places.

Obtructions

During its downstream journey a river will encounter features and obstructions that temporarily impede all or part of its flow, and during winter the contrast between areas of faster and slower moving water will be much more evident. While structures such as weirs, often

with accompanying lock systems, will briefly check the entire river, parts of the flow will frequently be slowed or diverted by such things as fallen trees (either fully or partially submerged), sections of the bank that jut out into the water, brooks and streams entering, bends in the river and the remnants of marginal weedbeds.

The Crease

Many species take up station on "the crease" between the two bodies of water. Here they can hold position comfortably on the edge of the flow without expending unnecessary energy, but quickly move out into the current to intercept any food items being carried downstream.

Crease swims not only attract a wide variety of species such as chub, roach, pike, perch and barbel, but can hold large numbers of fish on occasions, too. They are among the most productive swims to be found on a river and will provide consistent sport throughout the winter.

Avoid fishing areas where the surface is constantly boiling and churning. Caused by underwater debris, such water is disliked by fish as they find it uncomfortable, requiring them to constantly shift position and expend energy unnecessarily. Instead, look for smooth, evenly paced water.

ABOVE Quivertipping for chub and barbel beneath a partially submerged willow. The current will be slowed here by the tree's roots and branches.

FISH'N'TIPS

▶ *In winter, fish are most comfortable in smooth, steady-paced water.*

Stillwaters

STILLWATERS IN SUMMER

Stillwaters come in many forms, from small farm ponds, through old estate lakes, to large gravel pits and reservoirs.

Farm Ponds

Over the past 50 years, changes in agricultural practice have seen most farm ponds filled in and the land used to grow crops. However, those that still survive may not only offer some interesting fishing, but are often refuges for three rapidly declining species: crucian carp, rudd and the true wild strain of carp. Where they exist alone (or rudd with either of the carp species) there is then no chance of these species interbreeding with king carp, roach and bream, which they will all too readily do, resulting in hybrids.

Unfortunately, these three species often overbreed in a small pond environment, resulting in innumerable stunted fish that are all too willing to grab a hookbait – though for this reason they can be a good place to

BELOW Dam walls on estate lakes and reservoirs normally give access to the deepest water and during hot, sunny weather many fish will gravitate here.

introduce a newcomer to angling, with fast and furious sport guaranteed! Small ponds can sometimes throw up a surprise in the shape of a nice tench or even a big perch or eel that has waxed fat on the plentiful supply of small fish.

Estate Lakes

The lakes often found on large estates were usually created by the damming of a stream that ran through the landscape. All are generally triangular in shape, the narrower end being where the stream runs in, with the opposite, wide end consisting of a long dam wall, often with a central overspill weir to allow excess water to be released.

Many old estate lakes have slowly silted up over the years and are now relatively shallow throughout, though the water at the dam end will still be the deepest area. Although the margins on such lakes tend to shelve gently away into deeper water, the course cut by the old stream will often result in a deeper channel down the middle of the lake.

Traditionally, estate lakes were stocked with carp, tench and rudd, though today many also contain perch, pike, roach and bream. Eels often arrive naturally via the stream.

The muddy, silty bed of estate lakes usually result in lush weedbed growth in the form of rushes and lilypads, particularly around the margins, these are obvious features to fish alongside for tench and carp. It's worth noting that in estate lakes, tench will usually only feed when light levels are low – particularly at dawn – and will rapidly depart for deeper water once the first rays of sunlight of a new day strike the water.

Shallow estate lakes warm quickly in summer, and carp in them will often be seen basking at the surface. Carp will reveal their presence in many other ways, including bow-waving, leaping, head-and-tailing and rolling. Often, the very tip of their dorsal fin can be seen as they cruise around just under the surface. A tail waving above the surface in an area of shallow, muddied water will betray the whereabouts of a carp rooting in the lake bed for food. The inflowing stream will often prove an attraction to species like carp, both for its cool, oxygenated water and the food items that it washes into the lake – particularly during flooding.

Roach and bream are more likely to stay away from the margins, but will reveal their

location by rolling at the surface prior to feeding at dawn and dusk.

Rudd, particularly larger specimens, will also often be out in open water and spend much of their time at the surface, priming and rolling, as they roam the lake's acres.

Gravel Pits

Unlike estate lakes, the bed of gravel pits can be very irregular. This is due to the way in which the gravel has been extracted, yet the resulting uneven character of the bottom produces many fish-attracting features. The water in gravel pits is usually very clear enabling many features to be seen even

TOP Pole fishing the margins of stillwaters can be productive in summer, but most fish will move out into deeper water for the winter.

ABOVE Today, old "forgotten" farm and village ponds offer the best chance of finding three rapidly declining species: rudd, wild carp and crucian carp.

though submerged. Features to look for include raised gravel bars and the gullies between them, other raised areas of gravel manifesting as plateaux and sudden drop offs from shallow to deep water – many pits have a shelf around the margins along which carp and tench especially like to patrol in search of food. Spits or promontories on gravel pits are often associated with submerged bars, which many species like to work along.

If few or no features can be seen, it will be necessary to use a plummet to find them (counting down the time it takes to sink), which can be time consuming. However, plummets have been developed, that can speed up the mapping process and are available in tackle shops. Going afloat with a boat and fish finder is a much more efficient method and, if allowed, don't forget to wear a life jacket.

While bream prefer feeding over a clean

bottom, tench and carp can be caught on baits presented by and over weedbeds. If not visible, the presence of weed can still be determined by casting and retrieving a plummet or other weight on a braided (non-stretch) reel line. With practice it is possible to feel the character of the bottom over which the weight is being drawn. Birds such as coots and swans feed heavily on weed and will highlight its presence even when it is not visible. Furthermore, neither will descend far, indicating that the bottom is shallow where the weed on which they are feeding is growing.

Carp are very influenced by the wind and will move quickly to the downwind shore should a good breeze get up or the wind change direction. They are motivated by food brought in by the wind and carp will move into very shallow water in search of it – sometimes with their backs breaking surface.

While tench in old estate lake feed best at first light and shun bright sunshine, gravel pit tench will happily feed on the brightest and hottest of days, particularly when a breeze is also blowing.

BELOW Vast water-filled pits, created by the extraction of sand and gravel across the country for building materials, have transformed stillwater fishing in the UK.

BELOW An extensive planting programme and good management can rapidly transform a bleak gravel pit into a beautiful stillwater fishery.

LEFT During the summer carp and tench will use marginal lilies for cover and also feed on small aquatic creatures living on the stems and under the pads.

ABOVE During winter the branches of semi-submerged marginal trees will provide a perfect place from which pike and perch can ambush any passing prey.

In the summer, pit pike and perch will often be found close to the cover of marginal reed and lily beds where their camouflage makes them hard to spot. Also look out for fish-eating birds like grebes which dive for small fish and fry; perch and pike will not be far away.

Reservoirs

Reservoirs are large, man-made lakes principally constructed to provide a source of drinking water. However, one of the best reservoir complexes open to coarse fishing – Tring – was built to provide water for the adjacent Grand Union Canal. Some reservoirs are fed by streams, and fish are naturally attracted to them for their often high oxygen content (particularly during periods of hot weather) and the quantity of food items they carry.

Reservoirs used for holding drinking water will have points at which water is pumped in and drawn off; and they are usually marked by towers some way off shore. These structures attract many species, both prey and predator, and may sometimes be within casting reach of the bank angler. When not, it is often possible to hire a boat to be able to fish around them.

As with other types of stillwater, the wind is a key factor on reservoirs, and fishing into it in lieu of other assisting features is a sound policy for species such as carp, tench, bream and roach.

STILLWATERS IN WINTER

Winter fishing on pits, lakes and reservoirs is generally far more limited than on rivers. Most species will migrate into the deeper, warmer areas of a stillwater where they will remain until the spring, often out of reach of the bank angler. Going afloat is sometimes an option; usually the target for most anglers is predators such as pike, perch and zander, which follow the shoals of bait fish (roach, rudd, bream etc) into deeper water.

On estate lakes fishing from the dam wall into the deepest part of the lake – including the old stream bed – can be productive, while during periods of mild weather, when southerly or south westerly winds blow, carp will still respond by moving to the downwind shore of lakes and pits in search of food.

FISH'N'TIPS

▶ *Take photographs of gravel pits while they are still being worked. This will provide a permanent record of many fish-holding features that vanish from sight after flooding occurs.*

Canals

Extensive canal building began in England in the mid eighteenth century, initially as a means of moving coal to industrial centres and ports. Those still in use today have in many cases been restored, and are mostly used by pleasure craft traffic.

Canals offer good fishing for a wide variety of species even when they run through cities like Birmingham and London since their continuous towpath gives easy access to miles of water. They tend to be shallow and in summer warm quickly; the water in canals with little boat traffic becomes very clear and heavily weeded. Fish in this environment become wary, and are best approached stealthily with light tackle when light levels are low. In canals regularly stirred up by boat traffic, the water tends to remain turbid with less weed growth, and fish stocks are prepared to feed more confidently through the day.

Species

Some canals are connected to rivers at various points along their course, as for instance the Kennet and Avon Canal that runs through Wiltshire and Berkshire is to the river Kennet. Where canals are joined by rivers, they can be

LEFT *A popular spot! The water in canals used regularly by boats is usually permanently coloured, giving fish the confidence to feed right through the day.*

INSET *All species in canals are attracted to overhanging bankside vegetation and structures such as bridges for the cover they provide.*

BELOW *To avoid damage to tackle and possible confrontations, keep the towpath clear where it is in regular use by walkers, cyclists and joggers.*

LEFT *With their continuous towpath and frequent access points, canals offer many miles of convenient fishing in both rural and urban areas.*

BELOW *Perch are one of the species most commonly found in canals. In turbid water the perch's coloration will be much paler and the stripes less pronounced.*

quite fast-flowing, with beds of ranunculus (streamer weed), and contain additional species such as chub, barbel, trout and even grayling. The major canal species otherwise consist of roach and perch, with carp, bream, tench, eel and pike also present in many canals.

Location

In clear water canals particularly, fish will hold up close to whatever cover they can find, including weedbeds, under bridges, turning pounds, below lock gates and especially under moored boats.

Canal carp tend to be nomadic by nature but regularly baiting a swim can draw and hold them in an area where a hook bait can then be presented to them. This tactic has been used by a number of specialist carp anglers in recent years who have seen fish up to 40lb banked.

Eels in canals are attracted to areas that offer gloomy daytime cover, from which they

will emerge at night to feed. Holes and crevices found in crumbling brickwork, such as that at the base of bridges that cross canals, are favourite areas.

Canals attract more than just boats and anglers, and where they run through suburban areas in particular, towpath traffic can be heavy with joggers, cyclists and people just out walking. Towpaths can be narrow, so be wary of rods and poles obstructing them, avoid the risk of expensive tackle being ridden over or trodden on.

FISH'N'TIPS

▶ *For best results, fish early and late in the day, when boat and towpath traffic is at a minimum.*

Coarse Fishing Baits
Natural Baits

MAGGOTS

Maggots are eaten by every species and by fish of every size. They are available in a variety of colours and will also take flavourings well; adding garlic is very effective for chub and barbel. A sprinkling of maize or sawdust will help keep the maggots dry and in better condition, and they will survive longer if kept in a fridge.

BELOW Having a selection of baits enables different species to be targeted, or an alternative to be offered to fish that have become wary of fishermen.

If using one maggot, lightly nick it onto a small hook through the thick end. If using two maggots, hook the second through the pointed end to ensure neither can turn and mask the hookpoint. Always ensure the maggots are lightly hooked; should they burst on being attached, it is a sure sign the hookpoint has become blunt. Change it to improve bait presentation; it will also reduce the risk of losing any fish thus hooked.

CASTERS

Casters often account for a better standard of fish than maggots, and are frequently used in conjunction with other baits. Caster and worm or caster and sweetcorn are effective cocktails,

BELOW Bluebottle maggots are naturally white, but are dyed various colours by bait suppliers. Many anglers also add flavouring to increase take-up.

▶ *Lobworms keep best in damp newspaper that has been torn into strips and screwed up.*

▶ *Slugs collected but not required immediately will thrive on cucumber and melon.*

LEFT Although a major part of the carp's diet consists of bloodworms (midge larvae), they will take all manner of natural baits.

while loose-feeding hemp with caster as the hookbait is a successful combination for chub and barbel.

When used singly, casters are best presented with the hook completely buried inside. This is achieved by gently piercing one end of the caster and carefully threading it right over the hook.

LOBWORMS

Lobworms are great for catching most types of fish. They can be dug from the garden – easily collected from well-mown lawns on wet or damp nights with little wind. Use a dim torch as they are sensitive to bright light; tread gently and grab the worms quickly before they can shoot back into the ground down their holes.

BRANDLINGS

Brandlings are a smaller species of worm with yellow bands and a rapid wriggling action. They can be dug from manure heaps and are taken readily by species such as tench, rudd and bream.

RIGHT Like all cyprinid (carp family) species, bream are partial to cocktail baits; lobworms are often used in conjunction with maggots and casters but are also taken avidly on their own.

FISH'N'TIPS

▶ *Livebaits retained in a bucket will quickly exhaust the oxygen in the water. Change it regularly or use a small aerator pump (available from tackle shops).*

BELOW The majority of tackle shops offer a wide range of fast-frozen, fresh and saltwater fish. Fish baits can be dyed and flavoured to increase their effectiveness.

REDWORMS

Small redworms can be found in big concentrations in compost heaps. They make a good bait for many species.

SLUGS

Like lobworms, slugs emerge at night and can be found on lawns, flower-beds and footpaths as well as along the damp margins of lakes and rivers. In summer there is no more successful bait for chub. They can be fished on big hooks nicked through their thick skin and, being heavy, can be cast a long distance.

FISH BAIT

Live It is not only predators like perch, pike and zander that will take fish baits, but other species will also take them, including chub, trout, barbel and even carp.

ABOVE To save having to dig to collect lobworms prior to every fishing trip, introduce some to a compost bin or box where they will thrive and breed.

Effective small fish baits include the fry of any species, as well as stone loach, bullheads, elvers and brook lampreys. All of these are best presented on a single hook through their lips.

Quantities of minnows can be quickly caught by using a bottle trap baited with pieces of bread. These special traps can be bought from tackle shops. Again, minnows are at their most effective when lightly hooked through both lips.

Remember that, when casting with live fish as bait, they can only be used in the water from which they were collected. It is illegal to transfer them from one fishery to another. This law was put in place to reduce the risk of fish diseases being carried from one water to another. Please respect it.

Dead Most tackle shops offer a good selection of blast-frozen freshwater and marine fish baits. Depending on the time of year, supermarkets can be found that display mackerel, herrings, sprats, sardines, whitebait, rainbow trout and squid. Squid is effective for pike and catfish when fished whole or at around 6 inches long.

Bigger deadbaits intended for species such as pike and chub can be enhanced by being coated or impregnated with a concentrated marine fish oil using a big syringe. Often, when a pike first grabs hold of an oily deadbait, a slick will appear at the surface giving the angler an early warning of a run.

SHRIMPS AND PRAWNS

Peeled, boiled prawns are sold frozen in different-sized packs and are taken avidly by many species including trout, perch, chub, roach, bream and carp. Peeled prawns can be float-fished or legered whole, meanwhile loose-feeding with more prawns broken up into small pieces. Supermarkets also sell large tiger prawns, which, though expensive, will catch pike, chub and catfish.

FISH'N'TIPS

▶ *Whitebait make a highly effective bait for chub, successful in both stillwaters and rivers.*

Processed Baits

BREADCRUST

Breadcrust's buoyancy enables it to be used both as a surface bait and presented off-bottom over weedbeds and detritus. It can also be combined with other baits such as cheesepaste and worms. Such cocktail baits will not only often be more attractive to fish, but the combination can also produce a bait with a very slow sinking rate to land gently on weedbeds.

Chub and carp are enthusiastic eaters of floating crust and have big mouths capable of engulfing pieces as large as an inch square.

LEFT Breadflake is an excellent bait for chub; it can be freelined, trotted or legered. While fishing a swim, introduce free offerings to stimulate the fish into feeding, pressing the flake first to ensure it sinks.

FISH'N'TIPS

BELOW Mashed bread, made from stale brown and white loaves, is a great attractor and is normally fished in conjunction with breadflake hookbaits for chub and roach in winter.

For big-crust baits, use hook sizes between 2 and 6. Note that a dry piece of crust will double in size when saturated.

A piece of crust is best attached to the hook by being gently folded in half. Then thread the hook through both halves. When the crust is released it will unfold on the hook shank leaving the bend and point exposed.

When fishing a piece of crust on a freeline, dunk it in the water for a second before casting. Absorbed water will give it more weight, enabling it to be cast further.

BREADFLAKE

Breadflake is highly attractive to all members of the carp family and is often paired with other baits like sweetcorn and lobworms to form cocktails. It does not take long for flake to soften and break up in the water, potentially leaving the hook bare. Therefore, when legering pieces of flake, or float fishing them on stillwaters, it pays to recast regularly; this will also ensure a regular supply of free offerings into the swim.

When float-fishing flake on a river, strike off the hookbait at the end of each trot-through.

Flake is best mounted on the hook by gently folding a piece round the shank of the hook. This leaves the point of the hook clear, making

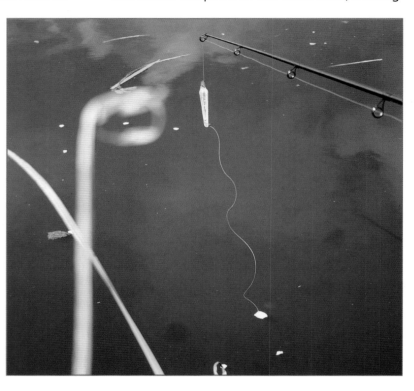

ABOVE Floating crust is an excellent summer bait for carp and chub. The best crust for hookbaits is found on the underside of an uncut white loaf.

missed bites less likely. For smaller species such as roach, rudd and crucian carp, a thumbnail-sized pinch of flake is appropriate and is best fished on hook sizes 10 to 14. When targeting fish such as bream, chub, tench and carp, however, the bait size can be doubled and fished on hooks between sizes 6 and 10.

PUNCHED BREAD

Bread punches come in a range of sizes and are most commonly used by match anglers to produce small bread hookbaits for species such as roach and dace. Punched bread can be particularly effective on low, clear rivers, and it is often used in combination with liquidised bread.

MASHED AND "LIQUIDISED" BREAD

In rivers, flake hookbaits are often fished in conjunction with loose-fed mashed or liquidised bread.

Mashed bread is best made from uncut loaves that have been broken up and stored somewhere dry for about a week to become really stale (fresh bread will not mash properly). These chunks should then be soaked in cold water until completely soft. As much water as possible is then squeezed out before the bread is mashed up.

Mashed bread is most commonly used as an attractor during the winter months for species such as chub and roach. Prepare a bucket of mashed bread at home. Not only will this be easier on your hands, but you will also be ready to start introducing feed to selected swims as soon as you arrive at the river.

Liquidised bread is, in fact, dry bread crumbs; the advantage that it offers anglers is that it is much lighter than mashed bread and is therefore easier to carry around in a bucket or bag. The particles are very small and of a uniform size.

Baiting swims with mashed bread or bread crumbs half an hour or so before fishing them with bread hookbaits often produces instant bites.

CHEESE

Soft and rubbery cheeses are better than hard, crumbly varieties as they can be rapidly mounted on the hook and, just as importantly, come off the hook more easily as a bite is being struck.

In winter, when the water is colder, cheese will harden up and at this time it is better to use cheesepaste to offer a softer bait.

MEAT

Luncheon meats with a higher fat content are more buoyant and useful for fishing over soft weed. Lower-fat meat produces a heavier, denser bait that will stay on the hook longer and can be cast further. Cubes of luncheon meat are often fished over a bed of attractor particles such as hempseed. Luncheon meat can also be coloured and flavoured.

Sausages, in a wide variety of sizes, flavours and colours, can be bought from most supermarkets and will be eaten by tench, carp, chub, barbel and catfish.

CAT AND DOG BISCUITS

These are buoyant foodstuffs that make excellent floating baits for surface-feeding species such as carp and chub. Dry mixers have accounted for hundreds, if not thousands, of carp over the years.

FISH'N'TIPS

▶ *Dice up luncheon meat before going fishing and consign the razor sharp-edged tin to a household bin to protect wildlife.*

▶ *Pet shops offer a wide range of processed meaty foods for cats and dogs, and carp also like them!*

LEFT *Cubes of luncheon meat are an effective bait for carp, barbel and chub. Low-fat brands stay on the hook better and can be cast further.*

Paste Baits

While some anglers still prefer to make up their own paste baits, for many others the recent arrival of commercially produced paste baits has been a godsend. Highly convenient, and readily available from tackle shops, these pastes come in a variety of flavours and colours – in floating and sinking forms – and can be used straight from the tub.

CHEESEPASTE

Cheesepaste should always have a soft consistency, and although it is usually made up with strong-smelling cheese in order to appeal to chub in particular, mild versions are also effective for species like roach.

Strong-smelling cheesepaste is not only ideal for chub, but it will also catch barbel, carp and even dace when rivers are high and coloured. The use of cheesepaste is often associated only with floodwater conditions, but it can be just as effective when rivers are running low and clear – a time when bread baits are generally considered a better bet. An excellent basic recipe involves mixing grated Danish Blue cheese with both white and brown bread crumbs. Sprinkle generously with salt (to enhance the flavours) and small amounts of fresh cooking oil and water. The cooking oil will help prevent the paste becoming too hard when fished in cold water. The entire mix should then be kneaded into a soft paste. Keep it refrigerated between fishing trips.

TROUT PELLET PASTE

An excellent paste bait originally used to catch carp, but one that appeals to many other species including tench and barbel. Place around a kilo of pellets in a bucket and just cover with boiling water. Leave for about half an hour for the water to be absorbed by the pellets. Drain off any excess water, add two or three raw eggs and any extra flavouring that is wanted. Everything should then be mashed up thoroughly. The eggs act as a binding agent and significantly slow the breaking down of the resulting paste.

SAUSAGE MEAT PASTE

Sausage meat is attractive to chub and barbel in particular. Mix with a binding agent such as sausage rusk, corn flour, maize meal or groundbait to stiffen it up to stay on the hook.

CAT AND DOG FOOD PASTE

Tinned cat and dog food – particularly the fish-based varieties – make good baits for species like carp, tench and catfish. As with sausage meat, pet foods are too soft to be used straight from the can and need to be stiffened up.

LEFT In the past, making up paste baits was a time-consuming process; now, however, they are commercially produced in a huge range of colours and flavours – as floaters or sinkers.

Boilies and Pellets

BOILIES

Boilies are widely available from tackle shops, produced in a variety of sizes from 6mm up to 25mm (sizes between 10mm and 18mm are the most popular) for targeting everything from roach to catfish.

Boilies are manufactured in a huge range of colours and flavours and as sinkers or floaters. Generally, sinkers are used both as hookbaits and free offerings while buoyant boilies – known as pop-ups – are employed in most cases as a hookbait only, and are usually fished just off a bottom that is clear of weed and debris.

PELLETS

Trout pellets are highly nutritious, generating rapid growth, and vary in size from crumbs, for feeding fry, up to one centimetre in diameter. They are available in floating and sinking forms and both types are rock hard. Mounting one on a hook is achieved by the use of a bait band (available from tackle shops), with bonding adhesive or by carefully drilling a hole through the pellet.

Owing to the huge growth in the use of trout pellets, custom-made fishing pellets are now available in a wide range of sizes and flavours. Some of these pellets are available pre-drilled for easy attachment, while in another development, a vast range of soft pellets are now available. These pellets offer the ultimate in convenience and can either be used on hair rigs or put straight on the hook. Smaller sizes are designed to be used either as a hookbait or as a carpet of free offerings over which a larger bait is presented – either a bigger pellet (possibly of the same type) or a completely different bait.

COATINGS

Sticky glutinous liquids, known as dips and glugs, are also now widely available and are designed for coating a boilie or pellet hookbait just prior to casting, to enhance their attractiveness. The viscous nature of these additives ensures they take some time to wash off. They are produced in an extensive range of savoury and sweet flavours.

ABOVE *Boilies have become a hugely popular bait for many species.*

ABOVE *Pellets are available in many sizes and in hard and soft forms, which allows different bait presentations.*

Seeds, Nuts and Berries

SEEDS

Hemp and Tares Hemp is generally used as an attractant, though it is also fished on small hooks (sizes 16 to 20) for roach, dace and chub.

Hempseed is very hard and needs to be soaked overnight, then boiled and simmered until around 50 per cent of the seeds have split, revealing the white kernel inside. When individual grains of hemp are used as hookbait, the hook is pushed into the split. Hemp would normally be fished on a float rig, and it pays to substitute the usual round split shot with oval samples, olivettes or lead wire. This avoids striking at false bites, as fish grab the split shot mistaking it for hempseed!

Barbel and carp love hempseed and are usually fished for with a larger bait presented over a carpet of hemp. Tares are larger than hempseed but are also hard in their natural form, and must be boiled after soaking until soft. Tares are usually fished singly on a size 14 hook – for roach, chub and dace – in conjunction with loose-fed hemp. Mount the berry on the bend of the hook with the point exposed. Hempseed is now available from most tackle shops pre-cooked in cans and plastic containers and in a variety of flavours.

FISH'N'TIPS

▶ *Sunflower seeds need no preparation and are loved by carp.*

▶ *Dye and flavour nuts for added appeal.*

BELOW Groundbait is produced in many colours and flavours, and can attract fish in its own right or carry small baits to swims beyond throwing range.

ABOVE Supermarkets stock many types of beans, seeds, grains and even prawns that make excellent and inexpensive baits.

Sweetcorn Sweetcorn in cans makes a superior bait to frozen corn since the loose grains are contained in a sticky liquid, which enhances the flavour of the corn. Corn is taken avidly by most cyprinid species, but when fished too extensively it can lose its effectiveness. Sweetcorn is now also available from tackle shops in a wide variety of colours and flavours as a change bait. It can be fished as a solo bait, or in conjunction with other baits such as bread, worms and maggots.

OTHER SEED BAITS

Many other seeds can be used as bait and especially for carp, tench and bream.

Those that are available in cans are pre-cooked and can be used immediately. All seeds purchased dry will need soaking and boiling first, to avoid damaging the fish's digestive system, as this can even result in their death.

Examples of other seed/particle baits include maize, red kidney beans and butter beans (soak for 24 hours before boiling) as well as maple peas, black-eyed beans, chickpeas, soya beans, wheat and barley (soak all these for 12 hours at least before boiling). Dry seeds are easily dyed and are flavoured during their preparation for use as bait. This can be done during the soaking process.

NUTS

The most commonly used nuts are tiger nuts and peanuts, with carp the most frequent target species. Soak them for at least 24 hours then boil for half an hour.

BERRIES

Elderberries are an excellent bait in late summer and early autumn for roach, chub and dace and are particularly effective where trees overhang the water. They are often used as hookbait, with hemp loose-fed as an attractor. Elderberries are soft when ripe, so hook them lightly to prevent them bursting.

FISH'N'TIPS

▶ *Elderberries can be preserved in formalin to prolong their use after the trees have shed their fruit. Rinse them thoroughly before using them.*

Artificial and Imitation Baits

In recent years the use of imitation baits has become hugely popular in coarse fishing for a wide range of cyprinid species. Their great advantages are that they don't break down in water and are immune to the attentions of small fish and crayfish.

The first available bait was imitation sweetcorn in natural yellow. However, versions are now produced in different colours that float or sink – and even glow in the dark!

Other imitation baits include maggots, casters, breadflake, shrimps, mussels, maize and boilies. As well as possessing a realistic shape and colouring, some are also impregnated with flavour to make them even more true to life.

ARTIFICIAL LURES – PLUGS AND SPOONS

Artificial lures are designed to catch predatory species and are made from a wide variety of materials including plastic, wood, metal and rubber.

BELOW Many natural and processed baits are now impregnated with flavouring to make them even more realistic.

RIGHT Carrying a selection of plugs, spoons and spinners in different sizes and finishes enables a variety of predators to be targeted.

FISH'N'TIPS

► *Buy old spoons from a jumble or car boot sale and make your own lures. Simply cut off the handles, drill a hole at each end of the spoon and add hooks, split rings and swivels.*

► *In low-light conditions, dark-coloured lures are usually more effective.*

► *Floating divers will work deeper if fished on thinner (but not lighter) lines.*

► *In spring and early summer, work jerk baits on and close to the surface to create disturbance and attract pike.*

SINKING PLUGS – DIVERS

Although some sinking plugs exhibit an almost neutral density and sink very slowly, most sink at the much faster rate of around 30cm per second. To work a sinking plug at a variety of depths, try counting as it drops before commencing the retrieve. Start off by retrieving after counting off a few seconds, and then on subsequent casts, gradually increase the time before you start to work the lure in.

FLOATING PLUGS – SURFACE WORKERS

Top-of-the-water lures create a surface disturbance to attract predators. Some are built with flat heads to displace plenty of water, resulting in a splashing, swirling action, while other models are fitted with small propellers to create an energetic churning and gurgling effect. For maximum effectiveness they should be fished very close to weedbeds, and can prove particularly effective on bright, sunny days when predators are reluctant to leave cover.

FLOATING PLUGS – DIVERS

Floating plugs dive when the retrieve begins. All are fitted with a plastic or metal lip (vane) at the head; its length and angle determines how deep the lure will dive. On some plugs the angle of the lip is adjustable to allow the lure to run deeper or shallower. With all floating divers, the faster the retrieve the deeper they will dive (down to their limit). Select patterns that resemble prey fish found in the water to be fished.

JERK BAITS

On many big waters, particularly on trout reservoirs, jerk baits have accounted for some huge pike. Jerk baits are large lures, available both in floating and sinking forms, that can be cast a long way. They have no inherent action of their own, with all movement having to be created by the rod tip. A series of jerks, twitches and taps of the rod tip will create the impression of a wounded or dying fish. Working jerk baits for pike is a demanding style of fishing that requires appropriately powerful tackle.

JIGS

Like jerk-bait fishing, jig fishing is gaining in popularity in the UK. Jigs are most commonly fished from boats, worked up and down near the bottom, and will account for pike, zander and perch.

SPOONS

Basically, spoons consist of a metal bar with a swivel attached at one end and a treble hook at the other. Spoons are produced in a variety of lengths, gauges and weights and can be either cast and retrieved or trolled behind a boat.

Spoons finished in gold, silver, bronze and copper will need polishing periodically to be at their most effective, while painted spoons are maintenance-free. Some are imitative, resembling prey fish, while others are brightly coloured so as to be seen at a distance or in silty water.

SPINNERS

Spinners are metal lures on which a blade rapidly revolves. Traditionally, the oval-shaped blades were given either a silver, gold, copper or brass finish, but today, spinners are available with blades in many other colour schemes including stripes and spots.

On some spinners, coloured beads are threaded on to the central stem and a brightly coloured wool-like material attached to the treble hook to be added attractors.

GROUNDBAITING

Groundbait is normally introduced into a swim just before fishing starts, with top-ups during the actual fishing session if required. It can be

LEFT Artificial breadflake and luncheon meat. A huge advantage of these baits is that they are immune to the attentions of small fish and signal crayfish.

LEFT Add hookbait samples to groundbait and deliver it into the swim by hand, catapult or swimfeeder.

introduced by hand, if the area to be fished is not too far out from the bank, with a catapult for more distant swims, particularly when the intention is to float-fish, or by means of a swimfeeder when legering the hookbait – often at long range.

Mixing groundbait properly is essential if lumps or the wrong consistency are to be avoided. If too wet and soft, the groundbait will break up prematurely – possibly even in the air on the way to the swim. If too stiff, it will lie on the bottom without breaking up. Groundbait introduced to a river will need to have a stiffer mix than for a stillwater so that it will get down to the bottom in one piece before breaking up. On a stillwater, on the other hand, the groundbait will need to break up quickly after reaching the lake bed to produce an attractive carpet of feed.

Baits like sweetcorn, hemp, chopped worm and casters can easily be mixed in to the groundbait, while old floating casters that have been crushed up will really enhance the mixture's attractiveness.

FISH'N'TIPS

▶ While mixing up groundbait, pause periodically and drop mini balls of it into the margins, checking the consistency by seeing how long they take to break down.

▶ To prevent diving ducks eating introduced groundbait, try to bait swims on stillwaters at dusk (or later) the night before fishing, when they won't see you.

▶ Groundbaiting with chopped-up fish can be effective for predators such as pike and chub – particularly if done for a number of days before fishing.

Coarse Fishing Tackle

With many different coarse fish species living in a wide diversity of environments, it is not surprising that the range of fishing tackle available is so extensive. Always ensure that the tackle selected is suitable for the intended task, and buy the best quality you can afford.

Rods

Trotting

BELOW Trotting rods are required to provide good float control and speedy line pickup, to enable fish to be hooked at distances of up to 40 yards.

Trotting rods are most commonly 13ft long and are designed for fishing buoyant fat-bodied floats like Chubbers, Loafers and Avons, down streamy glides, for distances of up to 30 or 40 yards. To be able to hit bites at this sort of range, then to tire and tame any larger fish hooked, trotting rods need to be robust and snappy in action like a waggler rod, but also possess sensitivity in the tip to absorb the lunges of any fish hooked in these fast flows. They are ideal for targeting roach, dace, chub and grayling and should be coupled with lines of between $2^{1}/_{2}$ and 4lb.

Longer trotting rods up to 16ft in length are now available that give improved float control and more effective line pick-up when striking over long distances. More powerful models

designed for catching big chub and barbel on the float are now being offered by some companies, too, and should be used with lines from 5 to 8lb.

Stick Float

Stick float rods are normally 12ft or 13ft in length, slim and lightweight. Fine-diameter tips with a crisp action allow rapid striking when used with light lines of 1½ to 2lb and even finer hooklengths.

Waggler Float

Waggler rods have a snappy action, but they also have cushioning in the top third of the blank to accommodate the long sweeping strikes required when fishing with a waggler setup. Use 2 to 5lb main line and lighter hooklengths, depending on species and bait.

Markedly different waggler rods are now being developed specifically for use on commercial carp waters, when fishing pellets up in the water under heavy floats. They tend to be shorter, at around 11ft, and are very light and comfortable to hold continuously while also regularly feeding the swim using a catapult. Responsive tip sections allow smooth and gentle striking for what can be

fast bites, while the flexible rod bends progressively as hooked fish try to escape.

Avon/Quiver

The Avon/Quiver is very probably the most popular rod in use today. It is certainly the most versatile, and it can be used to catch everything from dace to medium-sized carp and barbel.

Devised by John Wilson back in the early 1980s, Avon/Quiver rods are 11ft in length and through-actioned with a 1¼lb test curve, making them suitable for line strengths of between 4lb and 8lb. They consist of a butt section and come with two interchangeable tops. With the first, the rod becomes a traditional Avon and is suitable for freelining, float-fishing and bobbin-legering on rivers and lakes, while the second top section is designed for quiver-tipping and comes supplied with three or four (depending on the model) push-in quiver-tips with different test curves.

More powerful versions of the rod are now also available for carp and barbel; these and many standard Avon/Quivers are now also supplied with 2ft butt extension sections, taking them up to 13ft to gain improved float control on bigger rivers and for swims with extensive marginal weedbeds.

ABOVE This barbel angler is doubling up his chances with two rods, both equipped with quivertips.

Quivertip

Where once quivertip rods were available with just one tip that had a specific test curve permanently spliced in, today they come with a selection of push-in quivertips, each with a different test curve, enabling the rod to be used in a wide range of fishing situations and for a variety of species.

For big dace, roach and chub, which favour crease swims and living on the edge of the main current, use a light rod and quivertips with test curves of between 1 and 2½oz. For barbel and river carp, which usually live in stronger flows, a more powerful rod and stiffer tips of between 2 and 4oz will be appropriate in most circumstances.

On stillwaters, delicately biting roach at close range will require the use of a 1 to 1½oz tip, while targeting bream or carp at long distance using a heavy feeder will necessitate quivertips in the 2 to 4oz range, attached to a more robust rod.

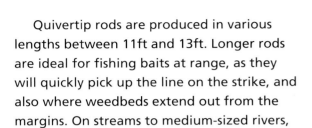

Quivertip rods are produced in various lengths between 11ft and 13ft. Longer rods are ideal for fishing baits at range, as they will quickly pick up the line on the strike, and also where weedbeds extend out from the margins. On streams to medium-sized rivers, rods of 11 or 12ft are fine.

A reel line of 6lb will cover most situations where you would use a quivertip. Increase the size of line where big barbel or carp are the target or snaggy conditions exist. Attach less heavy hooklengths for species such as dace and roach as well as for chub in low, clearwater conditions.

Leger

Leger rods tend to measure between 9 and 11ft and are primarily designed for use with some form of bobbin indicator positioned between reel and butt ring. Some models are fitted with a threaded tip ring to take a screw-in swingtip or quivertip. They possess Avon-style through-actions, and are best matched with lines of between 3 and 6lb.

Carp

Today, a wide range of carp rods are available with varying test curves and actions for targeting carp anywhere from the margins to well over 100 yards out from the bank. Most are 12ft long, of two-piece construction and very simply finished. Traditional, full-length handles are no longer in vogue and instead butt sections are fitted with just the reel seat, sometimes with a few inches of Duplon foam either side of it, and a longer length of Duplon at the bottom of the section for gripping during casting. Large, lightweight guides are fitted as standard to improve casting capacity, while run clips are attached just above the reel seat for bolt-rig tactics and to counteract windy conditions or an undertow.

BELOW John Wilson legering on the River Waveney with a modern version of the Avon/Quiver he designed in the early 1990s, regarded as Britain's most popular rod.

BELOW A pair of long-range carp rods with slim-line, non-slip handles and just a few large-diameter rod rings to minimise line resistance when casting.

Rods with test curves of between $1^3/_4$ and 2lb tend to be through-actioned and most suitable for close- to medium-range work. For medium- to long-range fishing, rods are available with test curves of between 2 and $2^1/_2$lb and middle-to-tip actions. For extreme distance, carp rods are produced with fast actions and test curves of between $2^1/_2$ and 3lb.

For anglers who enjoy stalking carp at close range from heavily overgrown banks, specialist short rods of between 8 and 9ft have been developed, with test curves of around 2lb. The blanks are through-actioned (bending progressively from tip to butt) to prevent either the hook pulling out when the fish is on a short line, or line breakages on the strike.

Predator

The most popular length rod for fishing live- or deadbaits from the bank for pike, zander and catfish is 12ft. They are available with test curves ranging from 2 to 3lb for use with lines of between 10lb and 15lb. Select a rod based on the intended fishing venue, the proximity of any snags, the size of fish expected and the weight of baits being used.

For perch and chub being targeted with small fish baits, a standard Avon or light carp rod coupled with 6lb line is fine. Use a wire trace if pike are present in the fishery.

All of these setups are also appropriate for wobbling deadbaits. Wobbling involves retrieving baits with a sink-and-draw motion in which they are made to twitch forward then allowed to briefly sink back, to imitate a sick or dying fish.

Lures (spoons, spinners, plugs etc) can be fished effectively from the bank with a standard Avon, carp or pike rod, as well as any snappy-actioned spinning rod between 8 and 9ft, depending on the target species.

Alternatively, custom-designed lure rods are available, ranging in length from 6ft to 10ft, that feature crisp actions for accurate casting. The shorter rods are often of one-piece construction, designed for single-handed casting, and sport crank handles for use with small bait-casting reels (multipliers). These are primarily for close-range work. Longer rods are normally fitted with conventional handles, and can be used with either a multiplier or fixed spool reel to fish lures at greater distances. Both types should be used with lines of between 10 and 12lb.

Shorter rods are preferable when lure fishing from a boat because of the limited space available and the constant casting necessary. However, the 12ft rods used on the bank for live- or dead-baiting are still perfectly adequate for boat-fishing, due to the fact that most of the time they will be lying static across the boat's gunwales, awaiting a run.

FISH'N'TIPS

▶ *The ideal line strength to be used with any rod can be quickly calculated by multiplying the rod's test curve by 5.*

BELOW With catfish in Britain having been caught weighing up to 100lb, and specimens in Europe at twice that weight, powerful rods are needed to land them successfully.

Jigging for stillwater pike, zander and perch from boats is becoming increasingly popular in the UK and specialised rods are now available. Jigs are small weighted lures that the fisherman works up and down in the water; these need a stiff-tipped rod to produce a lively action in the jig. Jigging rods are short – 6 to 7ft – and are best used with non-stretch braided lines to work the jigs effectively and also to hit bites in deep water.

Travel

Every year, an increasing numbers of anglers are going abroad to fish for a variety of species and, in response, many companies now offer multi-sectioned travel rods. As well as being highly convenient for use when travelling overseas, they can also be left out of sight and secure in the boot of a car, ready for spur-of-the-moment sessions. Telescopic rods are also useful when fishing on the move and take up very little space.

Poles

LEFT Although they are relatively light, long poles can be cumbersome. Pole rollers are used to smooth the process of shipping back a pole to re-bait or when playing a fish.

Although poles are available in lengths of 50ft or more, one measuring between 30 and 36ft is suitable for most pole-fishing situations. With better models, the sections are assembled by fitting the base of each upper section over the top of the section below. This system produces a uniform taper along the pole and continues to offer a tight fit between sections even if they wear over time.

Manufacturers normally recommend the range of elastic strengths that can be used with a particular pole, and usually supply spare 'top three' kits (the top three sections of the pole), which means that additional rigs can be made up with different strengths of elastic.

When buying a pole, ask the tackle dealer to rig the elastics of your choice through the top three sections.

Reels

Centrepin

The first fishing reels to be developed, centrepins consist of a line-filled spool rotating on a spindle or pin attached to the centre of a backplate. The spool revolves when there is the slightest pull on the line, enabling a float to be trotted down a stream or river both smoothly and under total control. The better models are produced from high-grade, lightweight aluminium; the spools often have a hollowed-out face with supporting spokes to the central pin, and holes are drilled around the edge to further reduce weight. Some reels have cutaway back plates for the same reason.

ABOVE A traditional-style centrepin reel, ideal for many float-fishing applications.

ABOVE The spool on a centrepin reel should begin to revolve at the slightest touch.

ABOVE A modern centrepin design with a cutaway backplate to further reduce its weight.

ABOVE Centrepin reels without line guards will cast float rigs further but are more prone to tangling.

LEFT A 2lb roach caught by trotting with a centrepin reel. Centrepins enable a float to be run down a river smoothly and under control the whole time.

FISH'N'TIPS

▶ *While line guards limit the casting distance of centrepins, they greatly reduce tangling around the backplate on windy days.*

▶ *If you forget to open the bale arm of a fixed-spool reel before threading the line through the guides when tackling up, just remove the spool from the reel, open the bale arm and then replace the spool.*

Centrepin reels with a diameter of 4½in are the best, since their size reduces the possibility of the line coiling as it leaves the spool, and they have a faster retrieve rate than smaller models. A spool width of an inch is preferable, so that as line is retrieved it can be spread across the spool, to prevent it digging into the coils below. Binding of the coils is most likely to occur when pressure has to be exerted on a bigger fish to bring it upstream, with the result that on the next trot down the swim, the float will not move freely as the line on the spool keeps catching. To further reduce the risk of the coils of line

snagging, centrepin reels should not be overfilled: you should need a maximum of 110 yards of line.

Most centrepins are equipped with an on/off ratchet and a sensitive drag system operated by turning a knurled wheel (milled to increase grip) on one of the spokes. This wheel can be used to slow the spool, and it enables a float to be held back sensitively as it progresses downstream. Fish can be played on a centrepin reel with great control by gently varying the pressure put on the revolving spool using the forefinger or thumb of the hand holding the rod.

RIGHT *Playing a fish on a fixed-spool reel. Correctly setting the clutch allows a battling fish to take line from the spool without any risk of the line snapping.*

Centrepins are also an excellent choice of reel when float-fishing close to the bank on stillwaters. If the rod is supported on two bank sticks, the reel's ratchet can also be put on to act as an audible alarm should a fast-moving fish, such as a carp or tench, tear away with the hookbait. Some river anglers do the same thing when using centrepins for legering at close range for barbel.

Fixed-spool

The spool only turns in fixed-wheel reels when line is being taken by a running fish. During casting and retrieving, the spool remains static.

When line is wound in as the reel's handle is turned, a bale arm rotates around the spool and feeds line evenly on to it. This bale arm is opened to free the line for casting, and is then closed again ready for bites to be struck and for the line to be retrieved. Because the line between the spool and bale arm forms a right angle, a free-running line roller is normally fitted to the bale arm to overcome line twist.

Fixed-spool reels feature a multi-adjusting drag system or slipping clutch, which on some models is sited at the front in the spool and on others at the rear of the reel. The clutch controls tension on the spool, and when set correctly will allow the spool to turn and give line to a hooked fish that bolts off, without any risk of the line breaking. The clutch should be set slightly lower than the breaking strain of the line, so that while the line won't break, a hooked fish will have to work hard for every

ABOVE *In recent years "Big Pit" reels with large-capacity spools have been developed to enable carp to be fished for at extremely long range.*

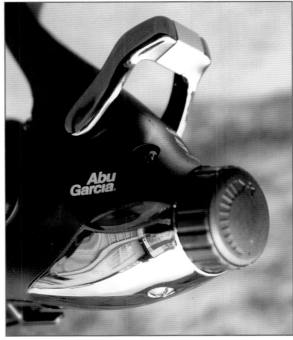

inch of line it takes. However, when the fish is under the rod tip on a short line, and it appears ready for netting, you should slacken off the clutch slightly more, for one last sudden lunge by the fish at this stage may see the line snap. When fishing overnight, check the clutch setting of your reels in the morning to ensure atmospheric conditions have not affected them – sometimes the weather can cause them to tighten up. Never leave rods unattended.

Some anglers prefer to play big fish by fully tightening the clutch or drag, which locks the spool, and then disengaging the reel's anti-reverse mechanism. (When engaged, the reel handle can only turn to retrieve line.) The angler then backwinds the reel handle to give line to a running fish. However, a sudden surge by a hooked fish can result either in rapped knuckles or an inability to backwind and give line fast enough, so that it will snap. The reel may well also overrun, causing the line to tangle around the spool, with the same result.

A fixed-spool reel's gear ratio describes how many times the bale arm will revolve around the spool and feed line on to it for every turn of the handle (e.g. 5:1). Higher gear ratios are found on match reels where a rapid retrieve is required between casts, while lower gear ratios are better for playing bigger fish and winding in with the line under load.

ABOVE The advent of fixed-spool reels revolutionised coarse fishing, making casting any distance a simple process, whether float-fishing, legering or spinning.

BELOW With rear-drag reels it is easy to adjust the clutch setting when playing a fish.

A huge step forward in fixed-spool reel design occurred in the 1980s with the advent of the free-spool or "bait-runner" facility. A lever at the rear of the reel is pushed forward to disconnect the spool from the drag mechanism, allowing fish to take line freely from the spool while the bale arm is still closed. A turn of the handle re-engages the drag mechanism at the pre-set level of tension for striking and playing hooked fish. Most free-spool reels have the additional benefit that tension can also be applied to the disengaged spool to combat surface drift and undertows. "Bait-runner" reels are most commonly used in conjunction with bolt-rigged baits, primarily for species such as carp and tench.

Over the years several models of fixed-spool reel have been produced specifically for competition anglers – the most famous being the Mitchell Match. These feature spring-loaded bale arms that open with a touch of the forefinger during casting. "Dab-bales" eliminate the need to open the bale arm manually prior to casting; these were designed to save anglers precious seconds during a competition.

Most fixed-spool reels are supplied with at least one spare spool, and additional spare spools can normally be purchased. This enables a range of breaking strain lines to be used with the same reel. Shallow spools are produced for fine lines, half-depth spools for medium-strength lines and deep spools for higher breaking-strain lines. A medium-sized reel with a selection of spools carrying 2lb, 4lb, 6lb and 10lb lines will make it possible to pursue a wide variety of species with the same setup.

Closed-face

Closed-faced reels were devised for competition fishing, using lightweight lines of 2 to 4lb, and as the spool is totally enclosed by a bell-shaped housing, they remain tangle-free even in very windy conditions.

Instead of a bale arm, a small pin revolves around the spool and feeds line on to it.

RIGHT Closed-face reels were developed for match fishing with lightweight lines. The spool is shrouded to prevent tangling in windy weather.

Depressing a button at the front of the spool retracts the spring-loaded pin for casting. A turn of the reel handle causes the pin to reappear and hold the line under tension for striking, retrieving and playing fish.

Some closed-face reels are fitted with an anti-reverse mechanism and a slipping clutch for playing fish, but with other less sophisticated models, backwinding is the only option when line has to be surrendered.

Multiplying

Multiplying reels are similar to centrepins in that the spool revolves; however, in a multiplying reel the spool is housed inside a cage or frame rather than on a backplate. Gears within the reel body multiply the number of times the spool revolves for each complete turn of the handle, whence comes the name for this type of reel.

Multipliers are used virtually exclusively in coarse angling for predator fishing. Small multiplying reels, often known as baitcasters, can be used from boat or bank for casting and retrieving small- to medium-sized lures, while for trolling big lures and casting heavy jerk baits from a boat, bigger and more robust models are necessary.

In the past, casting with a multiplier often led to overruns and bad tangles, as the speed of the revolving spool was difficult to control. Today, however, many reels are equipped with magnetic braking systems that slow the spool down. These brakes are easily adjustable and the spool can be released progressively to allow longer casting as proficiency increases.

Most small- to medium-sized multipliers are fitted with a level wind mechanism. This spreads line evenly across the spool as it is retrieved and ensures subsequent casts are smooth and problem-free. Some baitcasters are also fitted with an easy-to-use thumb bar which, when pressed down, disengages the spool ready for casting. The bar is designed to be depressed by the base of the thumb, while the top of the thumb clamps on to the spool and holds it still for casting. Turning the reel handle instantly re-engages the spool.

BELOW Large multipliers are tough and are used in coarse fishing for trolling big lures or casting heavyweight jerk baits from a boat, and when targeting big catfish.

Line and Hooks

ABOVE A carp hook
with a specially
shaped curved
shank to give
instant penetration.

ABOVE The carp
hook ready-rigged
with a neutral
density boilie
attached by a hair.

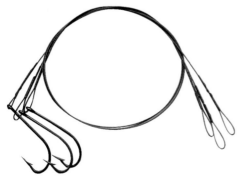

ABOVE Hooks can be purchased ready-tied
on monofilament or wire traces, although
many anglers prefer to trust their own
knots and crimps.

RIGHT Treble hooks
are used with lures
and fish baits for
pike. If using baits,
semi-barbless
treble hooks are
the norm, with just
one point barbed
to attach the hook
to the bait.

LEFT As fishing has become more sophisticated, numerous hook patterns have been developed to cater for different species, sizes of fish, baits and fishing methods. The type and number of barbs may be limited by the rules governing some waters.

LEFT Braided lines are supple and sombre in colour, and are used in the construction of many carp rigs.

RIGHT A properly filled reel will provide superior casting, since line will leave the spool with minimal resistance.

NOTE: Discarded and damaged line from a day's fishing should be taken home and then burned or cut into short lengths before disposal.

BELOW Co-polymer lines are very good in terms of breaking strain, and make excellent hooklengths when float-fishing for carp and for wary roach and chub in clear water.

LEFT When used regularly, reel lines should be replaced at least twice each year as UV light will weaken them. Bulk spools offer the best value, but store them in a dark place.

Netting and Weighing

RIGHT Large triangular landing nets with 42-inch arms and a deep mesh are favoured by big-fish anglers seeking carp, pike and catfish.

BELOW Round landing nets with a 24-inch diameter frame and a shallow mesh are ideal for barbel, chub, tench, bream and medium-sized carp.

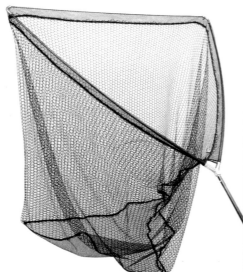

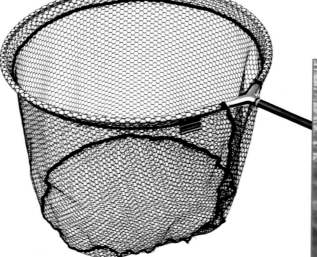

ABOVE Match anglers are the primary users of keepnets, with all fish caught during a competition being retained for weighing in at the finish.

ABOVE Stake out keepnets after use to dry off and let any fishy smell dissipate. Nets packed away while wet will stink!

ABOVE Use a landing net with a micromesh base to prevent fish – especially carp and barbel – from getting their fins snagged and damaged.

RIGHT Keepnets with a quick-release mechanism at the bottom enable fish to be released without having to lift the net from the water.

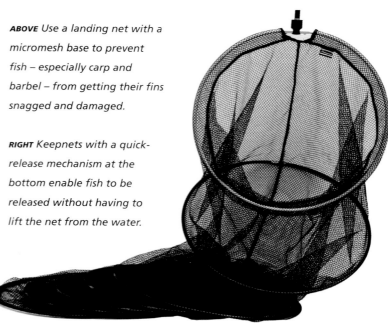

ABOVE Battery-operated electronic scales with a digital readout are quick to read and simple to use. Some can store details of every fish weighed.

ABOVE Dial or clock-face scales are favoured by big-fish anglers, as some models can weigh fish up to 100lb in 2oz divisions.

ABOVE To ensure spring balances operate accurately, it is important to keep the spring well oiled and free of rust.

BELOW Retain fish in sacks for short periods only, in shady spots in the margins, then release them as soon as possible.

RIGHT Weighing slings are made from soft nylon reinforced with webbing straps. Always wet them before placing a fish inside.

Floats

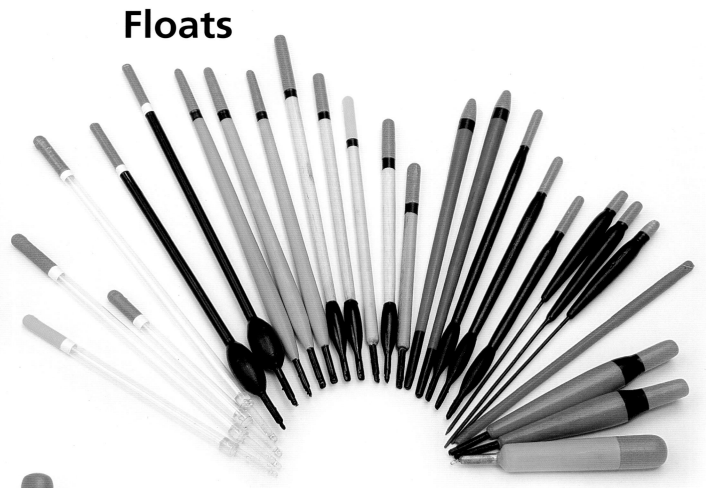

ABOVE Floats are available in many designs to enable a wide variety of baits to be presented naturally to many different species in a whole range of aquatic environments.

BELOW Floats are constructed from a variety of materials that best suit their purpose, including balsa wood, foam, wire, various reeds and canes, and plastic.

ABOVE Two modern "carp puddle" floats that cast far and will cock immediately on landing to indicate instant bites. The model on the left also carries groundbait.

ABOVE A selection of carp controller floats, used in conjunction with small buoyant baits which are too light to be freelined, to catch carp at the surface.

LEFT *A short piece of peacock quill – attached at the bottom end only – is ideal for float-fishing margin swims. Paint a batch with a range of coloured tops for use in different locations, since they are hard to see in low light conditions.*

RIGHT *Carry duplicates of every float used in case of loss; a range of coloured tops is useful, since certain colours can be seen more clearly in different light conditions.*

Weights

LEFT In-line leads are used in bolt rigs and are designed to pull free should a hooked fish become snagged.

LEFT The Arlesey bomb is the most commonly used leger weight and incorporates a swivel to prevent tangling when being cast long distances.

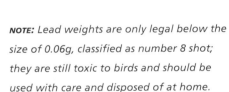

ABOVE Split shot is produced from soft, non-toxic materials; it can be removed easily from the line to be used again.

ABOVE AND ABOVE RIGHT Small- and medium-sized drilled bullets are ideal for cocking the large floats used in predator fishing.

NOTE: Lead weights are only legal below the size of 0.06g, classified as number 8 shot; they are still toxic to birds and should be used with care and disposed of at home.

RIGHT Large drilled bullets are used for rolling baits along snag-free riverbeds in search of fish.

BELOW Most split shot is sold in dispensers containing between four and eight different gauges, although small tubs of individual sizes are also available.

RIGHT To avoid damaging the line, split shot should not be pressed on too tightly. This also makes it easy to reopen the shot for repositioning or removing.

Pole Tackle

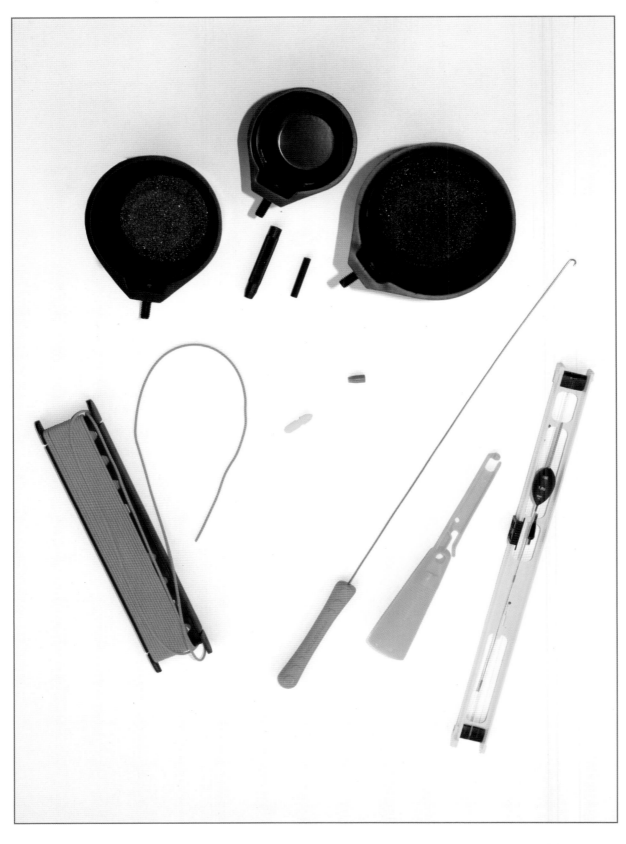

Feeding a Swim

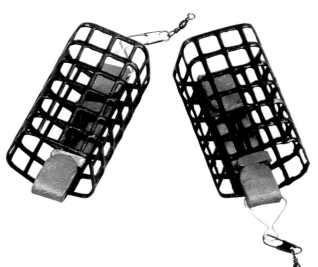

RIGHT Open-ended wire cage feeders are made to carry groundbait. Closed-block end-feeders have one removable end cap and are designed primarily for use with maggots.

BELOW Weighted cage feeders are employed for feeding at long distance. Clip-on leads are available to further increase the weight of any feeder.

RIGHT Clip-on pole cups enable extremely accurate feeding when pole-fishing. Attached near the tip, they are filled with bait, which is then deposited gently exactly where required.

RIGHT Catapults with vinyl pouches are used to fire out loose-feed baits such as maggots and hempseed. Groundbait catapults have rigid pouches to prevent the mix crumbling.

LEFT Catapults are used to accurately bait swims beyond throwing range, including when a headwind is blowing. Ultra-powerful models will transport boilies 100 yards or more.

Bite Indicators and Rod Supports

LEFT A hodgepodge of rod rests being used to support two rods.

ABOVE A multi-positional front rod-rest head designed for quivertipping or feeder fishing.

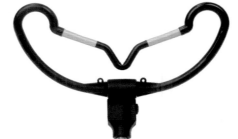

LEFT A high-sided front rod-rest head incorporating a quick-lock tilt facility.

RIGHT Most bite alarms incorporate a free-running wheel, which revolves when the line lying across it moves. This triggers an audible alarm and a warning light.

BELOW This angler is using extending bank sticks and "butterfly" rod-rest heads to support both rod and line clear of tall bankside rushes.

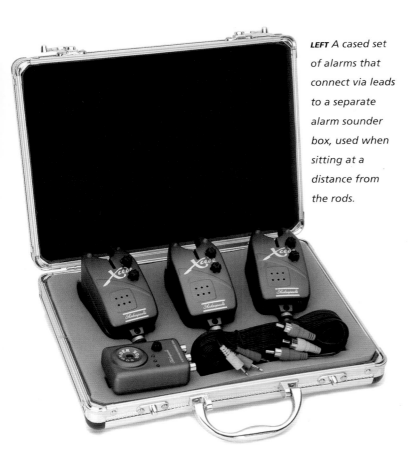

LEFT A cased set of alarms that connect via leads to a separate alarm sounder box, used when sitting at a distance from the rods.

General Accessories

BELOW Headlamps are extremely useful when night fishing: they leave your hands free to perform many tasks, including re-baiting hooks, tying rigs, and unhooking, weighing and photographing fish.

BELOW When quivertipping at night, illuminate the rod tip with a torch beam rather than stare at a small chemical light on the rod. Angle the beam upwards away from the water.

RIGHT When fishing for larger species such as carp, barbel, pike and catfish, always place them on a soft mat for unhooking to prevent injury. On many fisheries, their use is now compulsory.

ABOVE A good pair of polarising sunglasses will greatly reduce glare off the water, making it easier to spot fish near to the surface. Wear a peaked cap or broad-brimmed hat to keep the sun out of your eyes when fish-spotting or watching a rod tip or float for bites.

RIGHT Many species show at the surface either when feeding or when about to feed, basking or moving from one area to another. Binoculars are excellent for spotting them.

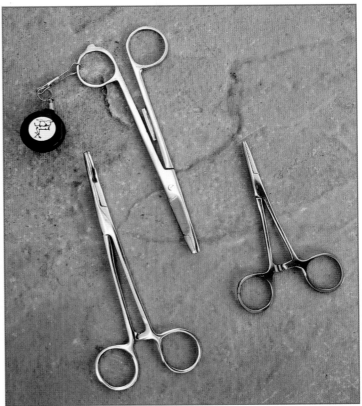

BELOW Versatile scissor pliers can both cut and grip. Combine them with a pin-on reel attached to a jacket or waistcoat to keep them close at hand. Stainless steel forceps with securely locking handles are perfect for removing hooks larger than a size 12. They are available in different lengths and come with straight or curved points.

ABOVE Disgorgers rapidly and cleanly remove small hooks from fish. Plastic models float if dropped into the water, but they also have a hole at the base to attach a cord.

ABOVE A fisherman's waistcoat is an excellent garment for carrying a host of accessories, as well as a folding landing net that can be hung from a ring at the side or the back of the neck.

Specialist Accessories

RIGHT Swivels prevent line twist and are used in the construction of many rigs. Snap-lock swivels (far right) enable the rapid substitution of leger weights and lures.

ABOVE Stiff, soft and shrink tubing is used in the construction of many carp rigs to enhance bait presentation and prevent tangling of the hooklength during long-distance casting.

ABOVE AND RIGHT Small, free-running beads, often made from soft rubber, are much used in rig making (particularly for their cushioning effect), and are also used between sliding floats and stop knots.

LEFT Bait bands are used to hold hard pellets, and plastic stops retain boilies on hair rigs. Sinking putty is used to provide weight, and cork balls are used with paste moulded around them to create neutral-density or pop-up baits.

RIGHT Should a fish become snagged, safety clips ensure the quarry will not remain attached to the leger weight and damage its mouth in an effort to break free.

RIGHT Baiting tools. Drills are used to bore holes through nuts and hard pellets. Short needles are used to attach single boilies to hair rigs. Long, or stringer, needles are used to thread a number of baits on to a link for free offerings.

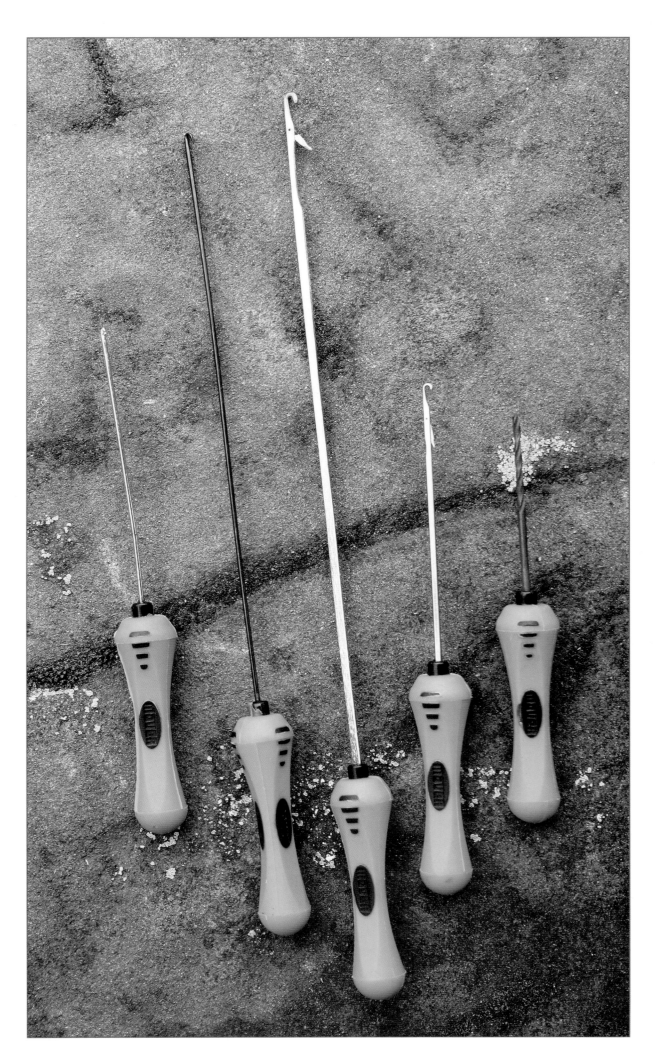

Pike Accessories

BELOW Most pike anglers prefer sliding floats because they can be used in deep water, and they also rapidly alter the depth at which the bait is presented.

BOTTOM Always use a wire trace when pike fishing. From the left: a stiff jerk-bait trace, a spinning trace and a semi-barbless snap tackle for live- and deadbaits.

RIGHT The use of a gag to hold a pike's jaws open during unhooking is discouraged these days, since it can do damage to the fish. Forceps are ideal for removing treble hooks.

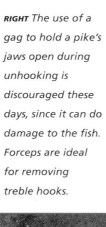

General Equipment

RIGHT Modern competition fishing boxes are functional, stable, strong and light. Many features come as standard, but extra accessories are also available, such as bait trays and pole rests.

BELOW Plastic tackle boxes are roomy, lightweight and robust. Accessory trays, seat cushions and adjustable legs to make the box level on any surface can be added.

ABOVE A long-stay specialist rucksack incorporating a free-standing frame and mud feet. The pockets are custom-designed to accommodate small pouches and wallets for holding bait and accessories.

BELOW Small accessories are normally allocated to the numerous pockets found on carryalls, with larger items such as waterproofs and food stored in the main compartment.

RIGHT A multi-section zipped and padded pouch containing six jars for baits or dips and elasticated loops to retain a range of baiting tools.

ABOVE Modern bivouacs come in various sizes. They are generally easy to erect and dismantle, and also give good protection from the elements.

BELOW Insulated boots will keep feet warm on the coldest of days. During the summer, wear breathable walking boots rather than wellingtons to prevent feet overheating.

LEFT Fishing umbrellas provide shelter from the wind and shade from the sun. It is essential to peg them down in gales to prevent them from being blown away.

RIGHT Bivouac features include double walls to prevent condensation, built-in groundsheets, front windows through which to view rods, and mesh doors to keep out mosquitoes.

Coarse Fishing Methods

Fish vary widely in where, when, how and what they eat; sometimes even the time of year will change the habits of a particular species. Some, like carp and chub, will seek out food at all depths, while rudd feed mostly at the surface and barbel close to or hard on the bottom. Over the years many different tactics have been developed, targeting individual species in a range of environments, and these tactics will be covered in this chapter.

Freelining

BELOW Freelining is a close-range method so always ensure you keep low and use whatever bankside cover exists to remain out of sight of your chosen quarry.

Stealthily moving along a riverbank in summer will often reveal groups of chub, lying virtually motionless at or close to the surface. The best bait with which to catch them is a slug. Chub love slugs, and the moment one hits the water near a group of chub they will instantly compete for it.

In any group of chub, individuals will vary in size. To improve your chances of catching one of the bigger specimens, try throwing in a few free bait samples to break up the shoal,

choose a target, then cast the hookbait at one of the biggest fish.

In conditions where chub are not visible, the line will need to be watched for bites. Most often the line will twitch before beginning to draw across the surface – strike as it does so. Where a cast has been made upstream, a biting chub will normally drop back with the bait, resulting in the line lifting or twitching then falling slack. Take up the slack before striking.

LEFT On warm, sunny days chub will bask quietly near the surface. Approach them stealthily from downstream and they will quickly engulf a freelined slug or lobworm.

following the crusts downstream. Sometimes the crusts will travel a fair distance before they are encountered by a group of chub, so don't give up!

To ensure your crust hookbait drifts downstream as naturally as the free offerings, the reel spool will need to be filled right to the lip and the line greased to make it float.

Carp love to work the margins of lakes in search of food, and freelining crust is a great way to catch them – particularly at dawn and dusk, when they are more active. Introduce a few free offerings and present the hookbait among them. Sit back from the water's edge and remain as quiet as possible.

Try draping the line just above the baited hook across a reed stem or lily pad to conceal it from the carp. If a group of carp of different sizes appear, delay lowering the hookbait on to the surface. Then, while they are actively feeding on the sample crusts, the hookbait can be carefully presented in front of the biggest fish.

Freelined floating crust is successful for summer chub. Target a moderate- to fast-paced section of river, throw in around a dozen crusts and watch them as they drift downstream. Chub will not normally be long in coming to the surface and will swirl and slurp at the free offerings. If no fish are seen, continue

BELOW In summer, freelining a piece of floating crust is an excellent method for catching carp as they patrol the margins. Introduce a few free offerings and sit well back.

Float Fishing – Rivers

While float-fishing on rivers is an enjoyable and effective method by which to search for fish, it is also challenging in that the speed and depth of the river constantly changes.

Fixed Top and Bottom

When fishing in fast, shallow flowing water, choose extra buoyant, chunky floats such as Chubbers and Loafers. These are available in a range of sizes, and with their broad tips, remain visible at distances of up to 40 or 50 yards. Attach them to the line at the top and bottom with wide float rubbers to reduce the risk of the float slipping when striking. This also makes it quick and easy to switch floats.

Bulk the cocking shot together about nine to twelve inches from the hook, then attach a smaller shot (a BB or less) about four to six inches from the hook, to take and keep the bait down near the riverbed. The shot's size

BELOW A trio of chub caught from a steadily flowing glide, on trotted breadflake fished below an Avon float.

BELOW In fast, turbulent water, baits are best presented beneath a large buoyant float with a highly visible broad top. Loafers and Chubbers are ideal for this.

and position will depend on the speed of the current and the depth of the swim.

In fast water, a lighter float will not result in more delicate presentation. It is better by far to use a bigger float, properly weighted, to achieve stability in the rig.

At the end of every trot through, stop the line and hold the float firmly in place for a few seconds before retrieval. This causes the bait to rise in the water, and this can stimulate fish into taking it.

During colder weather fish will be less active, and the speed of the float and bait will need to be slowed

ABOVE To be successful when float-fishing on rivers, it is essential to carry a good selection of float patterns to ensure effective bait presentation in a wide variety of swims.

down to increase the chance of bites. In really cold weather the float should be fished deeper than needed, with additional shot and with the float held back really hard right through its run down the swim.

Chubber and Loafer floats can be used to carry numerous baits. Small baits should be used on hook sizes 14 to 18 and lines of 2 to 3lb. For bigger baits, hooks should be increased to sizes 6 to 10 and lines to 5 to 6lb.

FISH'N'TIPS

▶ Floats fixed top and bottom can be prevented from slipping on the line either by twisting the line round the float between the two rubbers or by adding a third float rubber at the midway point.

Avon floats are normally used in waters that are less rapid and turbulent. They possess fat buoyant bodies with slimmer tips above and long, slender stems below. Some feature wire stems to provide greater stability in faster water. They are weighted and fished in a similar way to Loafers and Chubbers.

Stick floats are slim and parallel in profile and are used to trot baits through steadily flowing, even-paced water. Because there is not the need to get the bait down to the bottom quickly and keep it there, the shot are evenly spread out on the line between float

and hook. For balance in the rig during casting and fishing, the shot should reduce in size towards the hook. Stick floats are also available with stems made of wire and heavier woods such as lignum, to provide more stability in faster flows. As with Chubbers, Loafers and Avons, stick floats are not designed to be fished far out.

When trotting a stick float for dace, roach and small chub, a reel line of 2 to 3lb is fine. Couple it with hooks in sizes 14 to18 and with baits such as maggots and caster. However, when the water is low and clear and the fish

RIGHT Specimen dace caught from the swirling waters of a chalkstream hatchpool using a Chubber float. In slower, steadier flows an Avon or stick float would be a preferable choice.

FISH'N'TIPS

▶ *When a stick float is being blown off course by the wind, pinch a small shot onto the line either side of it. This will sink the line close to the float, reducing the effect of the wind and allowing it to fish steadily.*

depth in faster flows. Again, depending on the speed of the water in the swim, between one and four swan shot will need to be pinched on the line about a foot above the hook.

The baited rig is cast downstream and slightly out, and should be allowed to swing round in the current. Once the shots have settled, pay out a few feet of line to create a bow between float and weights. It is this bow of line that slows down the bite.

BELOW In cold weather, fish become lethargic and disinclined to chase after trotted baits. At such times, presenting a static bait on a stret-pegging rig can be highly effective.

ABOVE All floats designed for river work and attached to the line top and bottom are at their most effective when fished just off the rod tip.

are wary in consequence, it may be necessary to use a hooklength of a lighter breaking strain to get bites. Add on a 2ft length of 1½lb line and attach a size 18 to 20 hook to the end.

Stret-pegging is a highly effective method both in summer and winter. This involves presenting a static bait on the riverbed below a float attached top and bottom. Bites are very positive, and commonly consist of the float twitching prior to slowly sinking.

This method works best when used near bank crease swims. The float is fished below the expected depth – how much so depends on the speed of the current. It can vary between a few extra feet in slacker water to double the swim's

FISH'N'TIPS

▶ *Stret-pegging is an excellent method during floods when the lack of visibility forces fish to seek out food deep on the river bed.*

▶ *Try using a small waggler in shallow streams, as they make no disturbance when retrieved. Floats fixed top and bottom will flip over and splash about at the surface when reeled back upstream, risking spooking the fish you are trying to catch.*

BELOW Stret-pegging beneath a deep, undercut bank. Stret-pegging is particularly effective at night, when wary specimen fish usually feed more confidently. Use an illuminated float when night-fishing.

RIGHT A trio of chub taken on a waggler setup fished alongside overhanging far-bank trees.

For stability, the rod is positioned on two bank sticks to face downstream at about 45 degrees and is angled down towards the surface. The float should lie flat on the surface, and if it disappears or tries to cock, lengthen the line between float and hook. More weight may also have to be added, so experiment.

Stret-pegging can account for really big fish and is an excellent method when fishing after dark for wary specimens. Substitute the float used in the day for one fitted with a betalight or starlight.

Floats Fixed at the Bottom End Only

Waggler floats are most commonly used for fishing well out from the rod tip on slower-flowing rivers. A float fixed top and bottom will be continually pulled off the intended trotting line when the angler tries to control it at a distance. As the line is only attached to the bottom of a waggler float this will not happen, and this means they can be fished right across a river and run down close to weedbeds and overhanging trees.

There are two reasons it is important that the line between the rod tip and the waggler always floats. First, if the line sinks it will be affected by currents that will pull the float off target, and second, it is much harder to connect with bites when the line is sunk.

Most of the split shot used to make sure the waggler will cock is pinched on either side of the float. Known as bulk shot, it is used to lock the waggler on the line at a set position. When you go waggler fishing, particularly in the summer and autumn, bites may be expected on the drop as well as when the bait has reached its fishing depth, for the only shot on the line below the float are small and

evenly spaced, and cause the bait to sink slowly and seductively through the water. Bites on the drop will be indicated by the float failing to cock.

Wagglers can be used for fishing at distance in faster-flowing rivers, and here the float is locked in position by two smaller shots, with the bulk shot strung together nearer the hook to get the bait down quickly. An additional small shot is usually added between the bulk shot and hook to keep the bait down.

The baits, line strengths and hook sizes used in waggler fishing are generally similar to those employed with the stick float.

ABOVE Floats fixed at top and bottom are designed for use at close range. However, wading also allows mid-river and even far-bank swims to be effectively fished using them.

Float Fishing – Stillwaters

A wide range of floats have been designed for use on stillwaters. They can present baits from the surface right down to the bed, and from the margins to a long distance from the bank.

Floats Fixed at Bottom End Only

The big difference between waggler fishing on stillwaters and rivers is that on stillwaters the line is always sunk between the rod tip and float to overcome surface drift – a factor that will require long sweeping strikes to connect with bites. Four different types are used on stillwaters to cover a wide range of conditions and situations.

Straight Waggler These have a parallel profile from top to bottom and are ideal in flat calm and light winds at close to medium range. Use with a reel line of 3 to 4lb with hooks in sizes 12 to 14 tied directly on for baits

like bread, sweetcorn and worm. For maggots and casters choose lighter weight line with a 1½ to 2lb hooklength and size 16 to 18 hooks.

Insert Waggler A straight waggler with a slim tip section set in, designed for margin fishing and detecting bites from delicately feeding fish. Couple it with similar hook and line sizes to those recommended for the straight waggler.

Bodied Waggler These are fitted with a buoyant body near the base to provide extra stability in choppy conditions. They also have a greater weight capacity of up to 5 swan shot, enabling baits to be presented at long range. Use with reel lines of between 3 and 5lb and hooks tied direct; size depends on the bait or species.

Loaded Waggler These are weighted at the base so they require few additional shot to make them cock. Use them with buoyant

BELOW When waggler fishing on stillwaters, the rod tip should be positioned low after casting, to prevent surface drift affecting the float and bait presentation.

▶ *Rather than thread the line through the ring at the base of the waggler, which will hamper changing the float, push an easy-release silicon float adaptor on to the bottom of the waggler and thread the reel line through the hole in it.*

baits like bread and stale casters for a really slow sink rate to take fish on the drop. Use reel lines of 3 to 4lb with lighter hooklengths for small baits.

With all wagglers used on stillwaters, the bulk of the shot are locked on either side of the float. More shot are then attached further down the line – their positioning will depend on the bait used and any inherent buoyancy it might possess.

To get a bait to sink slowly and target mid-water species like roach and rudd, spread the shot out.

ABOVE Large-bodied wagglers enable fish to be caught on a float rig at long range.

LEFT Waggler types: from left to right, straight, insert, loaded and bodied.

For bottom feeders like tench and bream, position the lowest shot to rest on the lake bed. If unwanted roach or rudd intercept the bait on the way down, speed up its sink rate by moving more shot closer to the hook (about 10 to 12 inches away).

When planning to fish baits on the drop, count how long it takes for the shot to sink and the float to settle. When on any cast it fails to cock in the same amount of time, it indicates that a fish has intercepted the bait as it was sinking.

Casting Wagglers

Wagglers should be cast out with an overhead action for accuracy. Cast a few yards beyond where you wish to present the bait and gently slow the line by holding a finger against the reel spool just before the float lands. This action will ensure the hook and weights precede the float on splashdown to prevent the line tangling.

As the float lands bury the rod tip under the water and quickly wind in a few turns of line to tighten it up and bring the rig over the area to be fished. When the float's tip appears above

the surface raise the rod tip to a few inches above the water and support it on two rod rests. On rough days leaving the rod tip just submerged will keep the line out of the wind.

The Lift Method

The lift method is so called because as a fish sucks in the hookbait, it inadvertently supports the split shot pinched on close to it which cock the float. No longer anchored down, the float slowly rises – or lifts – from the water.

A length of peacock quill or a straight waggler are both ideal for fishing by the lift method, and should be attached to the line bottom-end only by means of a float rubber. The float is then cocked by split shot pinched on very close to the hook. Depending on the size of the float chosen, a single large shot may be sufficient to cock it. As the lift method was designed for use at close range, a large float should never be needed.

Bites are most frequently indicated by the float slowly rising then falling flat on the surface. The time to strike is when the float is rising, since the bait will be inside the fish's mouth at this point. Don't wait until the float

BELOW A brace of deep-bodied rudd. Loaded wagglers allow high-water feeders like rudd to be caught on the drop well out from the bank.

LEFT *When fishing using the lift method, strike as the float is rising, not when it subsequently falls flat on the surface, for at this point the bait is often rejected.*

FISH'N'TIPS

▶ *Because split shot weigh far less in water, adding extra shot to the lift method to stop small fish pulling the bait around will not lessen the rig's sensitivity or deter bigger fish.*

falls flat before striking, because at that stage the fish is completely supporting the weight of the shot, and the bait will be ejected.

The rig is best cast out with a gentle underarm flick. Being very close to the baited hook, the split shot will lead on the cast, allowing the setup to be cast out from between trees and bushes, and will land accurately in the gaps between beds of lily pads and in patches of surface bubbles caused by feeding fish. To avoid spooking the fish, cast just beyond the bubbles then slowly draw the float – and bait – back over them.

ABOVE *Tench are the species most commonly associated with the lift method, though it will work for any species that feeds close to the margins.*

RIGHT A chunky
common carp caught
on a floating pellet.
Controller floats
allow lightweight
buoyant baits to be
cast out at least
30 yards.

FISH'N'TIPS

▶ Although it might
be thought that, due
to the sensitivity of
the lift method, the
rod is best supported
on bank sticks, it is far
better to hold the
rod, as bites can be
lightning fast.

▶ Use clear plastic-
bodied wagglers
when targeting wary
fish in clear and
shallow water.

When targeting tench and bream with the lift method, use reel lines of between 3 and 6lb depending on the proximity of snags and weedbeds and the size of the fish present. For carp, increase the line's breaking strain to 10 lb. The distance between the shot and the hook is not an exact science and it is best to vary it until bites are registering properly. However, as a general rule of thumb, start off by setting the shot around 3 inches from the hook for tench and 6 inches for carp.

Although floating baits aimed at margin-feeding carp can be presented on a freeline, fishing them any further out will require some form of carrier. "Tenpin" controller floats fit the bill perfectly. They are available in a range of sizes and, being self-cocking, no further weight is required on the end rig. While smaller models are designed to transport floating baits around 10 to 15 yards out, larger sizes can be cast to target areas 30 or more yards away.

Rig one up by first threading the reel line through the rotating ring at the top of the float. Then thread on a small bead before attaching a lighter breaking strain hooklength anywhere between 2 and 6ft in length. When a carp takes the floating bait

it feels no resistance as the line runs freely through the eye of the float.

Unlike in all other forms of float fishing, when using a controller the bait must be watched, not the float. Remember, the float is only a carrier and will not disappear when a fish takes the hookbait. It is important to loose-feed samples of the hookbait to get the carp feeding confidently before casting out the hookbait. Once they are feeding, cast beyond the area in which the carp are feeding and wind the float and bait back carefully to avoid spooking them.

Hold the rod at all times but don't strike too soon when a take does come. Always wait for the line to start running through the eye of the controller to ensure the carp has taken the bait properly. Apply a grease to the line and hooklength to ensure they float, enhancing bite detection.

ABOVE Battling with a good carp. When using floating baits, first gain the carp's confidence by catapulting out loose offerings, and only then cast the hookbait.

ABOVE A common carp caught on the lift method using a short length of peacock quill for a float. Use 10lb line when targeting carp with this method.

Float Fishing – Pike and Catfish

The most frequently used pike float today is the slider, which can be used for a range of methods involving both live-and deadbaits.

To fish a sliding float, a small bead is first threaded on to the line and followed by the float. A stop knot, either made from a length of cotton or power gum, is then tied on to the line above the float. Any simple knot is fine but it needs to be tight enough on the line that the float and bead cannot dislodge it, but not so tight that it cannot be moved with a finger and thumb. Adjusting the position of the knot will dictate the depth at which the bait will be presented below the float.

A simple livebait rig will see the line below the float tied to a snap tackle (a wire trace and two treble hooks). To keep the fish down in the water, pinch split shot on the line just above the wire trace. This rig allows the bait to roam.

Float legering a livebait will restrict the bait's movement and is a good method for fishing baits close to snags and weedbeds. The set up is a paternoster rig with a snap tackle attached to the main line at a chosen distance from the leger weight below it, which dictates how far off the bottom the bait fishes. Attach the leger weight at the bottom of the rig to a lighter length of nylon. Then, if it snags, only the lead will be lost.

This rig is very effective in stillwaters and slow-flowing rivers. A good tactic for faster flows is to use a lighter lead that just fails to stay at the bottom. The livebait can then be slowly trotted down runs and glides, with the lead tripping along the riverbed.

RIGHT Played out and ready for netting. Sliders are the floats most commonly used by pike anglers for presenting both live- and deadbaits.

BELOW Held on a tight line, a defiant pike tailwalks across the surface. With strong winds forecast for later in the day, the angler's rig incorporates a drift float.

FISH'N'TIPS

▶ *Make livebaits stand out by attaching brightly coloured bait flags to the treble hooks.*

▶ *The float leger paternoster is also an effective setup for zander fishing.*

BELOW Catfish will take bottom-fished baits during the day but at night will also take those presented at the surface.

Drift floats incorporate a vane or sail that catches the wind and will carry a bait out for hundreds of yards. At these ranges, braided lines are a better choice than monofilament as they are non-stretch and float allowing the hooks to be set effectively over a long distance when a pike takes. With the amount of line that can be out on the water, it is important to use a reel with a big capacity spool loaded to the brim.

Catfish

While catfish are generally thought of predominantly as bottom feeders, they will come up higher in the water when searching for food, especially after dark. The dumbell rig was specifically designed for use with livebaits, and keeps them tethered at the surface where they splash around, creating catfish-attracting vibrations.

Legering

Legering comprises two basic methods: one in which the weight runs free; and one where it is fixed in position.

Running Rigs

The simplest form is known as the sliding link leger rig and is most commonly used on rivers for species such as chub and roach. It consists of split shot, lightly pinched on to a short piece of nylon line that has first been folded in half over the main line. This link runs freely on the line and is stopped from dropping all the way down to the hook by another split shot attached to the line at a set distance above it. When a fish picks up the hook bait it feels no resistance as the line runs through the loop in the nylon.

Although a simple rig, the sliding link leger is also versatile, since split shot can be quickly added or removed from the nylon loop to vary the weight of the link. This might well be necessary when roving between swims with different rates of flow, and where the distance to be cast varies. The other advantage of this rig is that if it becomes snagged for any reason, including by a hooked fish, the split shot will pull free of the nylon loop, leaving the main line and hook free.

RIGHT The link leger rig is ideal when its weight can be altered in seconds to reflect different speeds in the current.

BELOW Should a sliding link leger rig become snagged, only the split shot will be lost and not the hook.

One version of this rig can be slightly modified for use when a heavier weight than split shot is required. Thread a small ring on to the main line and attach a short length of nylon to it, then tie a quick-release swivel to the other end. Any weight of lead you need can then be attached to or detached from the swivel in seconds.

As with the basic sliding link leger, a split shot is pinched on to the main line to hold the running link above and away from the hook. It pays to use a lighter breaking strain line for this link in case it snags. Then, only the lead and not the hook (perhaps with a fish on it) will be lost. If the weight is too heavy, however, it will soon dislodge the holding split shot, resulting in the lead link sliding down to the hook. In this situation it is better to tie in a swivel as a replacement for the holding shot. Ensure a small bead is threaded on to the main line above it to prevent the small link ring and the swivel from locking together.

As a further modification, separate hook links of different breaking strains and sizes of hook can be tied up with a quick-release swivel at the top of each; these clip on to the lower eye of the swivel, stopping the running lead link, and enabling not only rapid change of the weight, but also of the hook length. This allows a variety of species and swims to be targeted quickly and easily without having to remove one complete rig and replace it with another.

When fishing with a sliding link leger rig, the usual length of the hook link would be between 18in and 2ft. However, when fish are feeding timidly, either due to intensive fishing or weather and water conditions, it can pay to increase the hook length by as much as several feet. This will reduce resistance and should result in more positive bites. Longer hook lengths also pay off when fished over soft weed, as the bait will sink more slowly and come to rest on the weed instead of being pulled down by the leger weight.

ABOVE Many anglers prefer to hold the rod while legering and feel for bites by looping the line over a finger, because not all bites will pull the rod tip round.

FISH'N'TIPS

▶ *When a fish is hooked among beds of ranunculus (streamer weed), get downstream of it and play it from this position. Apply constant pressure and it can be extracted easily.*

Conversely, when fishing big crust baits for chub, the sliding link should be stopped just a couple of inches from the hook. This results in thumping bites because, as a chub picks up the crust, it immediately feels the weight of the split shot, panics and bolts.

Because the weight will lead the baited hook during casting, sliding link leger rigs perform best when used for close- to medium-range work. Casting them any further will risk the hook length tangling with the main line.

Fixed Rigs

Fixed lead leger rigs are known as paternoster rigs, and differ from sliding leger links in that the lead weight lies alongside the hook length.

RIGHT When fish are feeding cautiously in cold weather, it can pay to reduce resistance in the setup by substantially increasing the hooklength.

FISH'N'TIPS

▶ Fish feel less resistance when picking up a bait legered upstream.

▶ Large split shot equivalent to 2 or 3 swan shot are ideal for use on a link leger rig.

ABOVE In fast flows, keeping as much line as possible out of the water between rod tip and leger rig reduces the amount of weight necessary to hold it at bottom.

LEFT Bream and roach caught using a simple paternoster rig. Substituting a swimfeeder for the leger weight enables free offerings to be introduced close to the hookbait.

This makes them more aerodynamic, allowing them to be cast further with less risk of tangling.

They are used both on rivers and stillwaters; when a fish picks up a bait fished on a paternoster rig and moves off with it, the rod tip or other bite indicator will show up the movement prior to the leger weight shifting.

One uncomplicated yet effective rig, for use on rivers for targeting species such as roach, barbel and chub, consists of the main line being attached to the top eye of a swivel (size 10) and the lead to the bottom eye via about 6 inches of nylon line. If the bottom is snaggy, the lead is best fished on a weak link, while attaching a link (instant release)

FISH'N'TIPS

▶ In snaggy swims plasticine or sinking putty can be substituted for leger weights.

▶ Wait for a confident pull before striking when touch-legering.

swivel to the end of this line makes changing the lead for a lighter or heavier one quick and easy. A hook length of about 2ft long is then attached to the top eye of the same swivel. A longer hook length may be necessary when fishing over weed or where bites are tentative – particularly from roach.

A modification of this rig involves tying a link swivel to the top of the hook length, as described earlier for the sliding link leger, to allow hook lengths of different breaking strains, attached to differently sized hooks, to be clipped on and off in seconds, enabling different species living in the same swim to

be targeted without radically altering the setup. Chub, roach and perch can frequently be found inhabiting the same swim, but each will require a different approach in terms of bait used.

Bolt Rigs

Bolt rigs feature extremely heavy leads, which create a lot of resistance to a biting fish, causing it to panic and bolt off with the bait and hook itself in the process. They are widely used to catch carp, bream, tench and even barbel.

This method is most effective with hard baits – especially boilies – that these species suck up then gulp back to their throat (pharyngeal) teeth for crushing and swallowing. Baits are usually side-hooked or presented on a "hair" to leave much or all of the hook exposed.

With hair rigs, the bait is not attached to the hook but is instead threaded on to a short length of line that hangs from it. When a fish sucks up a bait it also takes in the hook, and

BELOW A bolt rig setup ending in a hair-rigged boilie bait. Bolt rigs are frequently used to catch species such as carp, tench, bream and barbel.

BELOW Patiently awaiting some action on a gravel pit carp fishery. The bolt and hair rig combination has proved to be a devastatingly effective method for catching carp.

because the point is not masked by the bait it easily catches in the fish's mouth, virtually guaranteeing successful hooking.

Leads used for bolt rigs generally vary between 2 and 4oz. For general bolt rig fishing in stillwaters, weights of between 2 and 3oz are suitable ,while for barbel in strongly flowing rivers, flat leads weighing as much as 4oz may be necessary.

Inline bolt rigs are so called because the leger weight is in line with the fish as it moves off with the bait, leading to positive hooking. Should the rig become snagged and the line break, a hooked fish will not be left tethered because the line will pull through the lead. The 12- to 14-inch length of tubing above the lead protects the main line from abrasion, and also prevents the hook length from tangling during casting. A main line of 10 to 12lb is threaded through both it and the lead, and then attached to a size 10 swivel, which is then pushed into the lead for a snug fit. The hooklength is normally of soft braid and is tied to the other eye of the swivel; this should be 8 to 10 inches in length and with a breaking strain of between 12 and 15lb.

The helicopter rig is a bolt rig designed for use at long range. The hooklength is free to revolve around the reel line during casting; a combination of this and the 12 to 14 inches of silicone tubing threaded on to the main line above the lead prevents the hooklength from tangling. The hooklength should be 3 to 4 inches shorter than the length of tubing.

To set up the rig, first feed the reel line through the tubing then thread on a small rubber bead, a swivel and then a second bead. Slide them up on to the tubing, tie the reel line to the ring or swivel on the lead then push the tubing down over the swivel/ring and knot for neatness. The hooklength is tied on to the other eye of the swivel positioned between the two beads. Ensure it rotates freely for the rig to work properly. The breaking strain of the main line and hooklength are similar to those used for the inline bolt rig. Hook sizes for both rigs will depend on the bait used.

Competition anglers have adopted the bolt rig principle in recent years as more and more commercial stillwaters have been stocked with carp. The most commonly used setup is the method feeder rig, in which a large framed feeder is fished in the same way

ABOVE An average size gravel pit tench taken at long range on a paternoster rig that incorporated a heavily leaded open-ended swimfeeder and red maggot hookbait.

FISH'N'TIPS

▶ *Search for chub and barbel with a light leger rig that just fails to hold the bottom and rolls the bait through the swim.*

BELOW *A typical carp fishing setup, with a pair of rods fitted with free-spool reels, and both bobbins and electronic alarms to signal a bite.*

as an inline lead. The feeder is encased in a groundbait mix containing all sorts of fish-attracting items, from pellets (whole and ground) to nuts and seeds. The hooklength is kept short at 8 to 10 inches, to ensure the hookbait lies close to the groundbait-covered feeder. Actually burying the hook bait right inside the mix has two benefits. Firstly, the

hook bait is situated right where the carp's attentions will be concentrated, and secondly, locking in the hooklength prior to casting eliminates the risk of it tangling.

Block-end inline swimfeeders also work on the bolt rig concept. They cast well and are less prone to tangling than feeders fished on a conventional paternoster rig.

LEFT A hot, windless day and a flat calm lake. Tough conditions, but with baits in the water there is always the chance of a fish.

BELOW A light breeze begins to ruffle the surface. As it strengthens, carp will begin to move, especially to the downwind bank, in search of food.

LEFT Putting the line under tension, by attaching a bobbin in front of the reel, ensures that drop-back bites will also register and trigger the alarm.

Pole Fishing

Fishing with a pole enables a float to be closely controlled at all times and the bait below it to be presented with great delicacy. For maximum comfort and control when pole fishing it is essential to be seated on a rigid tackle box that is set level.

The weight of the pole is supported by resting it on the right thigh (assuming a right-handed angler) with the right forearm lying on top of it, holding the butt down. The right hand grips the pole from above. The left arm rests across the left knee with the left hand supporting the pole from underneath. Bites are struck when the pole is lifted with the right hand.

When groundbait is being introduced to the swim, the pole should be wedged between the knees, with the left hand again supporting it from underneath. The right hand is used to throw the groundbait, and any bites are struck with the left hand.

When firing out bait with a catapult, the handle of the catapult is tucked under the left leg and the pouch filled with the left hand. The right hand and forearm are supporting the pole. The filled catapult is

BELOW Unshipping the lower sections of a pole. Usually just the top three or four sections are held to land fish or re-bait the hook.

BELOW Where the depth of water being fished is less than the length of the pole being used, lower sections will need to be removed to enable fish to be landed.

then taken with the left hand over to the right, and the forefinger and thumb of the right hand take hold of the tab at the rear of the catapult pouch. The other three fingers of the right hand and the right forearm continue to support the pole. The catapult is then drawn forward by the left hand, extending the elastic. Now the catapult is under tension and is ready for firing. To do so, the right forefinger and thumb release their grip on the tab. Should a bite occur, it is struck by the right hand.

The amount of line used with a pole is dictated by the depth of the swim being fished. Normally about 2 to 3 feet of line is allowed for above the float, plus the distance between float and hook (the rig). When fishing only a short distance out from the bank, it may not be necessary to use all the sections of the pole. In swims further out, where the depth is considerably less than the length of the pole,

lower pole sections will need to be shipped behind you, then the top three or four sections removed and held, to enable fish to be swung to hand or netted, and also to re-bait the hook. Whether you are left holding three or four sections will again depend on the length of the line being fished – both line and pole should be of similar length. In deeper water, where a much longer length of line would be used, fish may be brought to the net or hand without needing to break down the pole. Again, the total number of sections being used would be dictated by the length of the line.

Rivers
Although mostly used by match anglers for catching small to medium-sized fish, poles can also be used to great effect by river anglers seeking larger specimens. Typical situations would include fishing beneath overhanging

ABOVE *When fishing deep swims, fish can be netted or swung to hand without the need to remove any lower sections of the pole.*

FISH'N'TIPS

▶ *When purchasing a pole, discuss with the tackle dealer where you intend to fish, so that they can advise you on the correct tackle to use.*

far bank trees and bushes, in the pockets of slack water found behind mid-river bulrush beds, and increase swims that are well out from the near bank. In all these examples, the pole enables the baited rig to be placed carefully and extremely accurately without creating any disturbance. For maximum control, always keep the pole tip directly above and a little way upstream of the float.

Conventional river floats can often be used with a pole in situations where bigger fish are the quarry. However, a huge range of floats specifically designed for pole fishing are also available, and the best course of action is to seek advice from a local tackle dealer on the most appropriate use in any given situation.

Stillwaters

On stillwater fisheries, just as on rivers, the hook bait can be placed quietly and accurately in the desired spot time after time. In addition, the close proximity of the pole tip to the float enables wind and surface drift to be successfully countered.

RIGHT A huge haul of roach and bream taken pole fishing on a deep-water lake. Calm conditions close in ensured trouble-free float control and effective bait presentation.

LEFT When fishing with a pole, rest it on the right thigh and hold down the butt with the right forearm or hand.

ABOVE Using a pole cup to feed a swim with great accuracy. Poles allow the float and bait to be repeatedly placed in exactly the same spot.

When fishing on stillwaters, bites can often be induced by gently raising then lowering the pole tip. This causes the bait to lift from the bottom before enticingly falling back towards it again.

Whips

Whips are short poles, normally telescopic and no more than 23ft long. They are most commonly used on canals, with fine lines, small floats and tiny hooks, and because they are designed for speed fishing for small fish, no internal elastic is required. Instead, the rig line is attached to a quick-release connector at the tip. Any small fish caught are swung straight to hand, while the ultra-slim tip of the whip will cushion the lunges of any bigger fish hooked.

Lure Fishing

The most productive time of the year for lure fishing is summer into early autumn, when water temperatures are at their highest and predators are most active.

Surface lures are fantastically exciting to use for pike. As a surface lure splashes and gurgles across the water, pike will appear from nowhere to attack it in a welter of spray. On many occasions pike will actually miss a surface lure – sometimes two or three times in succession – before finally grabbing hold of it. Don't strike at any surface disturbance.

Instead, just keep retrieving until you feel the weight of the pike on the line.

Fishing along the edges of weedbeds is the most productive tactic for catching pike on surface lures, so work a lure along the margins where reeds and lily pads grow.

During summer, fishing with sub-surface plugs, spoons and spinners may be hampered by excessive weed growth on some waters. With all predators being more active at this time, a faster retrieve can be used with metal lures, and this will also see them fishing higher

RIGHT A superb zander caught on a soft rubber lure weighted with a large bullet lead. On big stillwaters, zander will often be found feeding on bait fish in deep water.

FISH'N'TIPS

▶ Always use a wire trace when fishing for perch, chub and zander in case a pike grabs the lure.

▶ In rivers, perch and pike will often lie out of sight under overhanging trees. To target them, try trotting a floating diving plug downstream and past a likely looking tree or line of trees, then wind the lure back upstream right underneath them, where the predators lie.

LEFT To be consistently successful at lure fishing it is essential to carry a varied selection of lures – including duplicates in case of losses – in a range of colours.

in the water. Spinner and buzz baits, with their hooks protected by weed guards, are a good choice at this time. Where plugs are concerned, choose floating, shallow divers to fish clear of weed.

When fishing a lure, many anglers will unconsciously speed up the retrieve towards the end of the cast. This can be a problem, as pike in particular will often follow a lure for some distance and, when it speeds up, strike, believing their prey is about to escape. A pike smashing into a lure right under the rod tip can be a truly heart-stopping experience, and it pays not to have the reel's clutch set too tightly, otherwise the line may snap.

Sub-surface lures should also be fished close to weed beds, both along the margins and out from the bank, as well as around any other features such as landing stages and snags.

When working a sub-surface lure, vary the speed of retrieve and also occasionally flick the rod tip hard, which will cause the lure to jerk forward then fall back. All these actions will create the impression of an unwell or dying fish providing an easy meal for a predator. Ensure that the line between rod and lure remains tight at all times to prevent any missed takes.

Spinners are excellent for perch, although sometimes the fish will repeatedly follow but not bite. When this happens, attaching a worm to the treble hook will often result in positive bites.

Chub can generally be caught on floating plugs at dawn and dusk in summer and autumn.

BELOW With their large single hooks, spinner baits can be worked through extensive beds of lilies – where pike like to lie – without snagging.

Good numbers of zander are now present in Grafham Water and Rutland Water, where they live out in the deep water. Big catches – including some huge individual fish – are now being made at both of these reservoirs by boat anglers using jigs and shads as well as flies.

During the winter, predators can still be caught on lures, but when the water is colder they are much less active and the speed of the retrieve needs to be slowed down, with the lure fished closer to the reservoir bottom.

ABOVE To avoid damage to angler and fish, use a gloved hand to hold pike and remove hooks with a pair of long-handled forceps.

Dead fish are a good alternative to artificial lures on snaggy waters where tackle losses can be high. Both freshwater and marine species can be used – sprats are an excellent choice – and can be mounted on the same snap tackle that would be used to present live- and deadbaits under a float. Weight can be added by pinching on split shot above the wire trace.

Deadbaits are most successful when worked with a sink and draw action. Here the bait is retrieved in short jerks, between which it is allowed to sink back for a few seconds, imitating a wounded or dying fish. Keep the line tight at all times so it is easier to detect bites, although sometimes a bite can be surprisingly savage!

LEFT Perch are voracious predators and are often caught on large lures intended for pike. A small spinner with a lobworm attached to the treble hook works very well.

LEFT The optimum times to lure-fish for chub are at dawn and dusk through the summer and autumn months. Takes can be surprisingly aggressive.

While pike may look fierce, they are in fact delicate creatures and great care needs to be taken when handling and unhooking them. Always lie them on their side or back on a soft mat for unhooking, and with big fish, drape a damp towel over them leaving just the head exposed. Hold down the towel by kneeling with a knee on either side of the pike to prevent it from moving. Carefully slide two fingers under the gill cover on the underside of the jaw while the thumb is pressed on to the outer lower jaw. Then, slightly raise the pike's head and its mouth will open. With forceps in the other hand, quickly and carefully remove the hook or hooks. Special piking gloves are recommended to avoid any injury to pike or angler.

This unhooking procedure should be used for pike caught on both livebaits and deadbaits.

Fly-fishing for Coarse Fish

The coarse species most commonly targeted with flies is the pike, and on some waters pike have now been taken over 30lb.

Fly-fishing for pike mainly takes place during the summer and early autumn, when they are at their most active. Although pike can be caught from the bank on flies, going afloat allows more water to be explored with bigger and heavier fish-imitating flies, which can be up to 5in long and tied on size 4/0 hooks.

BELOW Going afloat when fly-fishing for pike enables far more water to be explored. A standard trout reservoir lure outfit is suitable.

A wire trace should always be used when fly-fishing for pike. One with a breaking strain of 20lb is fine, coupled with a line of between 12 and 15lb that connects to the fly line.

On late summer evenings stillwater and river chub will readily rise to take sedges and moths, and in autumn, daddy longlegs (crane flies) are blown

FISH'N'TIPS

▶ *Many gravel pits bordering rivers see mayfly hatching every spring. Any chub present will feed on the nymphs and adult insects.*

▶ *Many coarse fish include items in their diet that can be imitated by an artificial fly.*

on to the water. Use flies tied on hook sizes 8 or 10, depending on the pattern, and 6lb line.

With their upturned mouths, rudd spend much of their time feeding at or close to the surface, and can be caught on small dry flies, nymphs and buzzers fished high in the water. Fish flies in sizes 14 to 16 on 2lb breaking-strain line should be successful.

Dace, too, will rise readily to the dry fly – the Black Gnat in sizes 16 to 20 being an effective pattern – fished on a really light line of 1 to 2lb. It is important to note that dace will take and reject a fly with lightning speed.

Although imitation sedge and moth patterns do work, anglers who fly-fish for carp often use a floating pellet, dog biscuit or breakfast cereal like puffed wheat instead. Then, free samples can be catapulted out to get the carp feeding confidently before the hook bait is cast among them. Attach the chosen bait to a size 8 to 10 hook with a bait band, and grease the line to keep it on the surface for effective striking.

Many reservoirs which offer trout fishing on a day-ticket basis also hold huge stocks of coarse fish. Over the years some very big perch and bream have been caught accidentally from these waters on deep-fished nymphs and buzzers intended for trout.

Grafham Water, and its neighbour, Rutland Water, have also begun to produce zander in recent seasons in both quantity and quality, caught by boat anglers fishing out over deep water with lures on fast-sinking lines.

ABOVE A chub caught on a Pheasant Tail Nymph. Chub include all kinds of underwater life forms in their diet, like fly larvae and pupae, small fish, shrimps and snails.

GAME FISHING

Game fishing encompasses the pursuit of salmon, sea trout, trout and grayling. While lures and baits are frequently used to catch all these species, game fishing is most often associated with fly fishing.

Whereas in coarse and sea fishing a float or leger weight is used to carry the bait out into the water, in fly fishing it is the line that is weighted to transport the fly.

Fly lines are produced in weights from 1 to 12 to cover all forms of fly-fishing, from pursuing small wild brown trout in tiny streams, to casting for salmon in wide and powerful rivers.

They are made with two basic profiles or tapers. Double taper lines are slimmer at both ends, gradually increasing in diameter towards the middle. They are designed for delicate and accurate casting at short range. Weight-forward lines have most of their weight at the front end of the line and are designed for medium- to long-distance casting.

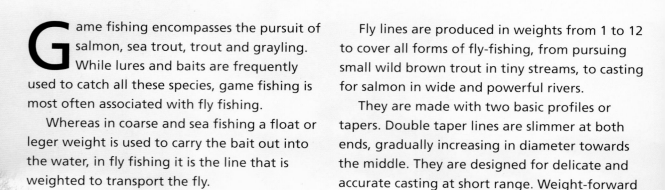

LEFT Wading for grilse (returning salmon) in high summer on a small spate river. On such waters, greater success will often be achieved by using small trout wet flies rather than salmon patterns, and wading gives greater access.

Fly lines are also produced in different densities, from floating to ultra-fast sinking, which descend at a rate of about a foot per second. Today, most fly lines have a loop attached to the end for tying on a leader or cast – the length of nylon that connects fly line to fly.

Fly rods are produced in a wide variety of lengths, but all are rated for use with a specific weight of fly line. For trout fishing, fly reels should be capable of holding a fly line and 100 yards of 20lb backing line. When fly-fishing for salmon, a reel able to carry a fly line and 200 yards of 30lb backing line will be necessary. Backing line acts like a safety net for powerful fish and will often run further than the length of the fly line.

When buying a fly-fishing outfit from a tackle dealer, ask for the reel to be loaded with the required fly line and some backing line, with a leader loop attached if there is not already one on the fly line. Dealers are also very likely to have a list of local APGAI (Association of Professional Game Angling Instructors) members who will provide casting lessons. The technique of casting a fly line is not difficult to master but is best learned from a professional. Fly fishermen who teach friends often unconsciously pass on their own faults.

MAIN PICTURE In early spring, trout will often be in deeper water, and require a sinking line to reach them.

ABOVE A magnificent brown trout caught during high summer on a floating fly line and a small dry fly.

Game Species
Salmon
Salmo salar

Atlantic salmon spend most of their adult life in the sea but spawn in freshwater – usually in the same river from which they originated. When they arrive back at their "home" river, salmon are magnificent, streamlined creatures sporting gleaming silvery flanks below a steel-grey back. Salmon run in clean rivers throughout the British Isles, although their numbers have declined in recent years due to overfishing at sea.

Salmon returning to spawn after one year are known as grilse and usually weigh between 3lb and 8lb, while those that stay at sea for two or three years before heading back to the river of their birth are now called salmon and normally weigh between 6lb and 20lb. A few salmon survive the rigours of spawning and return several times to breed. Atlantic salmon can weigh up to 60 or 70lb, but any salmon over 20lb can be considered

FISH'N'TIPS

▶ *Fresh-run salmon and sea trout can sometimes be difficult to tell apart. While the salmon's tail is slightly forked, sea trout possess straight-edged tails.*

▶ *The presence of sea lice on a salmon will indicate that it is fresh in from the ocean.*

ABOVE Salmon fishing on the River Feale in south-west Ireland. Salmon journey upriver to their spawning grounds when rainfall brings a rise in water levels.

a true prize. The British record stands at 64lb and was caught way back in 1922 from the River Tay.

Once embarked on their journey back to freshwater, salmon stop feeding and rely on their fat reserves to sustain them until spawning time. On arrival at their home river mouth they will await a flood of freshwater after rain before ascending, to ensure a sufficient depth of water in the river. During periods of little rainfall when rivers run shallow, large numbers of salmon can build up in an estuary and become vulnerable to attack by seals.

Depending on the length of the river, obstructions and water levels, it may take the salmon some time to reach the spawning grounds. Over this period in freshwater the salmon's silvery flanks become dull, then redden. Male salmon show a much darker coloration and also develop a large hooked

lower jaw called a kype. Close to spawning time the males become increasingly aggressive and, if caught then, both sexes should be carefully returned.

Salmon spawn between October and December in stony or gravelly shallows. The alevins that hatch from the eggs evolve into fry, then parr, and finally smolts, in a process that can take up to six years. Smolts develop silvery sides before migrating down to the sea then out into the Atlantic off Greenland, where they feed voraciously on small invertebrates and fish and grow rapidly.

ABOVE A silvery spring salmon. Newly arrived from the ocean, salmon are often carrying sea lice which drop after a few days in freshwater.

Sea Trout
Salmo trutta

BELOW While sea trout in rivers are generally wary during the hours of daylight, they can sometimes be tempted with a small dry fly.

Sea trout are a migratory strain of brown trout that live in the sea and, like salmon, only return to freshwater to spawn. Generally, sea trout originate from less fertile rivers and migrate to sea to take advantage of the richer feeding there. In contrast to salmon, sea trout do not venture far when at sea and normally remain within about 12 miles of their home river. Sea trout will also occasionally feed in freshwater, unlike salmon, and will sometimes be seen rising and taking flies during a prolific hatch.

Sea trout occur in coastal waters all the way around the UK and Ireland, though the species has suffered greatly in recent decades from the effects of numerous salmon farms sited inshore and often near river mouths, particularly on the west coasts of Scotland and Ireland. The caged salmon attract huge numbers of parasitic sea lice, and while the salmon are doused with chemicals for protection, the lice also attach themselves to any sea trout in the vicinity, seriously

weakening and usually killing them. Commercial netting of estuaries for sea trout also takes its toll, while their staple food of sand eels are now netted in large quantities, to be converted into pellets for feeding to farmed trout and salmon.

However, rivers in coastal areas not affected by salmon farms will often experience good runs of sea trout. The rivers of Wales in particular provide superb sea trout fishing, with individual fish weighing into double figures, while those in the West Country and many of the chalkstreams of southern England also enjoy substantial runs of sea trout annually.

Like salmon, sea trout resemble bars of silver when they first enter rivers to spawn, and as with salmon, become progressively more coloured the longer they remain in freshwater. However, unlike salmon, sea trout do not require an increase in water height to encourage them to run. They are prepared to move upriver even when levels are very low, and at such times tend to run at night for security. Larger fish tend to run in May and June, followed by far greater numbers (but much smaller fish) during July and August.

As with salmon, sea trout spawn during the winter and will return to their home river to spawn many times. They can live for up to 20 years.

The current British record weight is 28lb 5oz 4dr.

LEFT A splendid sea trout caught from an estuary on a bar spoon. Sand eels make up a significant part of a sea trout's diet while in saltwater.

FISH'N'TIPS

▶ *Never consider a water too insignificant to hold sea trout, for they will run the smallest of streams.*

▶ *Sea trout are most likely to run low rivers on warm and cloudy moonless nights.*

LEFT Sea trout colour up on entering freshwater, and in time will resemble any resident brown trout. In dark, peat-stained fisheries the transformation can be rapid.

LEFT When returning to a river from salt water, sea trout resemble bars of silver, take flies, lures and baits aggressively, and fight incredibly hard when hooked.

Brown Trout
Salmo trutta

Brown trout are indigenous to the UK and Ireland, occuring naturally both in rivers and stillwaters. In rivers wild brown trout rarely exceed 4lb, but in the large lakes of northern England, Scotland and Ireland they can grow to over 20lb. These monsters live for many years, feed predominantly on small fish and are known as ferox (ferocious) trout. Because of fishing pressure, many waters containing wild brown trout are now also stocked with farmed fish to provide consistent sport.

LOCATION

Many large reservoirs and lakes, set up as commercial trout fisheries, are stocked with farmed brown trout in lesser numbers than rainbow trout, due to the brown's slower growth rate (making them more expensive to rear) and poor tolerance of high water temperatures. However, farmed brown trout will grow larger, particularly those introduced into food-rich chalkstreams and fertile reservoirs in the Midlands and the south of England.

Brown trout always blend in with their environment for camouflage, leading to wide variations in colour. Those occurring in clear rivers and lakes usually sport light silvery yellow or silvery brown flanks, and a scattering of black spots that can vary widely both in size

BELOW Netting a slim, early season brown trout. Warm spring days will see trout rising to take hatching insects, such as olives and sedges, off the surface.

LEFT A big brown trout caught from a southern chalkstream. Brown trout introduced to fertile rivers and lakes will thrive and, if not caught, grow to specimen size.

and quantity. In marl (chalk-bottomed) lakes, like Lough Carra in the west of Ireland, the trout are very silvery and more reminiscent of sea trout, while those living in dark, peat-stained lakes and rivers tend to show dark grey-brown or even black coloration. Brown trout have very few, if any, spots on their tails.

Brown trout are territorial by nature, though this side of their character is more evident on rivers where they will hold station in a favourable lie and feed on whatever the current carries them. On lakes, brown trout are more prepared to travel in search of food.

FEEDING

The brown trout's diet is extensive and includes the larvae of many insects such as mayfly, sedges, midges and olives that live on the lake or riverbed, as well as the adult insects hatching or egg laying at the surface. Brown trout will also feed on a wide variety of other aquatic creatures including shrimps, crayfish, snails, hoglice and small fish, while wind-blown terrestrials, like daddy-longlegs (craneflies) that land on the water and worms washed in during floods, will also be taken.

WEIGHT

The British record wild brown trout weighed 31lb 12oz.

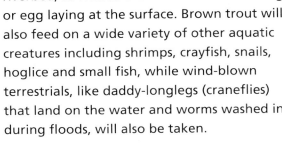

FISH'N'TIPS

▶ When a good brown trout is caught from a river, its lie is normally quickly taken by another trout.

▶ Brown trout are active surface feeders after dark, preying particularly on sedges and buzzers.

LEFT Like chameleons, brown trout blend in with their environment. The silvery yellow flanks of this brown trout indicate that it was caught from a clearwater fishery.

Rainbow Trout
Oncorhynchu mykiss

Originating from North America, rainbow trout are widespread throughout the UK but only as stocked fish. They have never successfully bred in this country apart from a few rare exceptions like the Derbyshire River Wye and the River Chess in Buckinghamshire, and live for a maximum of four or five years.

LOCATION

Rainbow trout stocked in large reservoirs are normally introduced at weights of between 1 and 2lb, but in those fisheries offering rich feeding they will grow rapidly, with some reaching double-figure weights. Reservoir rainbow trout in the peak of condition are lightly spotted bars of silver, with silver flecks in their tail fin and a pale pink flush on either flank. These fish fight incredibly hard as well as acrobatically, making screaming runs and cartwheeling across the surface in their bid to escape.

BELOW A warm smile on a cold day. Stillwater fisheries stocked with triploid (sterile) rainbows provide year-round sport and trout that are always in excellent condition.

Many rainbows stocked into smaller lakes are introduced at much higher weights, with individual fish well over 12lb and sometimes even heavier. They also tend to have far more spots, with more pronounced pink stripes running down their sides than on grown-on reservoir rainbows. Most fish in these small "put and take" fisheries are quickly caught and replaced from on-site cages or by regular deliveries in tankers.

Rainbow trout stocked in rivers often seem unable to forage for food in the way that brown trout can, and therefore fare less successfully in this environment. In their natural habitat in North America, many rainbows migrate to the sea to feed and then return after several years to spawn. Sometimes weighing 20lb or more, these fish are known as steelheads and are similar to reservoir rainbows in tip-top condition. Just occasionally, a sea-run rainbow is caught

from a UK river and usually gives its captor the fight (or fright) of his life!

Although unable to spawn in British waters, rainbows will still come into spawning condition during the winter and early spring. This sees them take on a progressively darker red-brown coloration, in particular the males, which also grow hooked lower jaws known as kypes. However, today such fish are becoming much less common as most fisheries stock with triploid rainbows, which are sterile, and remain in excellent condition throughout the year.

FEEDING

While rainbow trout will eat a wide range of aquatic creatures including shrimps, insects (larvae and adults) and small fish, on many waters their diet consists predominantly of bloodworms or daphnia.

LEFT Rainbow coloration varies widely, from copious spotting on the body and fins with prominent pink stripes, to virtually spotless silvery flanks and just the lightest flush of pink.

RIGHT Fin perfect: a small wild rainbow trout. Rainbows breed successfully in only a handful of UK rivers.

FISH'N'TIPS

▶ Rainbow trout are a shoal species so where one is caught others will be in the vicinity.

▶ Dull, overcast days will see rainbows high in the water, searching for food. On bright days they will feed at depth.

Grayling
Thymallus thymallus

Grayling are an oddity. The adipose (fatty) fin just above the tail shows them to be a member of the salmon family, yet they spawn in the spring, as do coarse fish.

LOCATION

Although very occasionally found in stillwaters, grayling are naturally a fish of fast-flowing cold water and in the UK are thus at the southern limit of their range.

Grayling are found throughout the UK but not in Ireland, and distribution is totally dictated by water quality. Grayling only thrive in the cleanest rivers and are highly intolerant of pollution. An early indicator of water quality problems in a pure river or stream will be the rapid demise of a healthy grayling population.

Grayling are most common in the waterways of Scotland, Wales and northern England, while populations also occur in some West Country rivers. They are also to be found in southern England in the cool and pure chalkstreams of Berkshire, Wiltshire, Dorset and Hampshire.

HABITAT
Grayling are very distinctive in appearance, with silvery grey scales overlaid with a violet sheen and a huge dorsal fin (larger on males), which they use to hold station in fast flows. Small black spots are scattered down the flanks. Grayling prefer to live in fast, shallow glides, though some larger specimens will seek deeper and more sedately flowing water, where they expend less energy waiting for the current to bring food down to them.

Grayling are a shoal fish, but in summer and autumn their numbers can be quite small. Winter frosts and cooling water sees them forming much larger groups.

FEEDING
For a fish with such a delicate appearance, grayling can be very aggressive feeders. Their large mouths are easily able to engulf fry as well as mayfly nymphs on the riverbed and hatching or egg-laying adults at the surface. They will also feed on many other aquatic creatures including shrimps, snails and the larvae of many insect species, though it is their liking for salmon and trout eggs that in the past saw them persecuted on many game fisheries. Thankfully, today many owners and keepers, recognising the value of grayling as a sporting species, are happy for them to be returned to the water.

WEIGHT
Any grayling over 2lb can be classed as a specimen though the current British record stands at a colossal 4lb 3oz.

ABOVE Male and female grayling, showing the much larger dorsal fin of the male. Grayling use their sail-like dorsal fin to hold position in fast flows.

FISH'N'TIPS

▶ Unlike most species, grayling are willing to feed after heavy frosts.

▶ Grayling writhe in the hand when being unhooked, but avoid gripping them tighter to prevent harm.

Salmon Fishing Methods

Fly-fishing on Rivers

As salmon don't usually feed in freshwater, they have to be provoked, or their old feeding response triggered, to make them take a fly or lure.

During the spring and late autumn, when water temperatures are below 10°C (50°F), fly-fishing for salmon is normally practised with a sinking fly line, for fish will be lying at depth. Once water temperatures rise over 10°C (over 50°F), salmon become more active and are prepared to come up in the water to take a fly, so flies can then be fished on floating or intermediate lines.

On large rivers, long and powerful double-handed rods are necessary for the water to be covered effectively. These rods most commonly

BELOW Spring fishing on Ireland's River Shannon, making use of a line of rocks built out into the river to enable a known salmon lie to be reached.

BELOW On bigger rivers double-handed rods, measuring between 13 ft and 15 ft, are used to cover the water effectively and give better control of the fly.

LEFT *Small spate rivers rise and fall quickly after rain and the taking time for catching salmon can be shorter.*

FISH'N'TIPS

▶ *Wading can be an advantage on big rivers but always wear a life jacket.*

▶ *Carry a 24–26in Gye net on your back. It is thus out of the way but is ready for use in seconds.*

measure 13ft and 15ft and are rated for 9- to 11-weight fly lines. Large-capacity fly reels carrying plenty of backing line are essential, for salmon are powerful fish and can make long runs in fast currents.

On smaller rivers, 10ft single-handed rods rated for 7-weight fly lines will comfortably handle any grilse hooked. Match them with a fly reel capable of holding 100 yards of backing line under the fly line.

During the spring and autumn, when large flies are used, the breaking strain of the leader should be between 15 and 20lb, and be slightly shorter than the rod. In summer, small flies will be more effective: attach a leader of similar length with a breaking strain of 8- to 10lb.

Flies for sunk-line fishing are rarely less than three inches long, and are often constructed from inch-long metal tubes with treble hooks below. Summer flies are much smaller and are normally tied on single or double hooks in sizes 8 and 10. On many small rivers, trout wet flies in sizes 12 and 14 are actually more effective than salmon patterns. Popular salmon flies include Ally's Shrimp, Stoat's Tail, Willie Gunn, Garry Dog and Munro Killer.

The optimum conditions for catching salmon on a fly are after a flood or spate when the river is dropping and clearing. Start at the head of a pool or run and cast about 45 degrees downstream and across the current. The fly should then be allowed to swing round to the near bank. Bites can come at any point, including close in at the end of a cast, when the fly should be left to hang in the flow briefly before being retrieved. After each cast, move two or three steps downstream until all the likely salmon-holding water has been covered.

Fly Fishing on Stillwaters

BELOW A morning's catch from a Hebridean loch. Employing a ghillie to quietly work the boat over productive lies using the oars will greatly increase the chances of salmon being caught.

Many Scottish and Irish salmon rivers run through lakes on their way to the sea and salmon will often hold in them for a time on their upstream migration. Salmon will follow the same course through a lake year after year, with the route often taking them from one headland to another; anglers trolling lures for them will take advantage of this fact.

When in lakes, salmon like to lie in shallow, well-oxygenated water where currents are quickly created by the wind, the conditions you would find in a river. Salmon are to be found along the lake margins among stones and boulders and around islands and reefs. They will often give away their presence by jumping, splashing and rolling, particularly those fish that are newly arrived.

FISH'N'TIPS

▶ *Cast flies really close to the shore, for salmon will lie in mere inches of water.*

Salmon can be caught from the shore, though a very stealthy approach is necessary if they are not to be spooked. They are more commonly fished for from a boat, drifting side-on to the wind, because going afloat enables far more water to be explored.

For two anglers to both be able to fish productively, it pays to have a third non-fishing person aboard, to control the boat with the oars and ensure it drifts quietly and effectively across the shallows, leaving the two anglers free to cover all the likely lies.

Usually a team of two or three wet flies are fished on a 10½ or 11ft single-handed rod rated for a 7-weight line. During the cooler months of spring and autumn, an intermediate line will fish the flies a little deeper, and will also hold the flies steadier on rough days at any time of the year. Through the summer months, it is better to use a floating line. In a big wave, flies tied on size 8 and 10 hooks will be spotted more easily by salmon, while during a period of light winds and a surface ripple, fly size should be reduced to size 12 or 14. Tie them on a 8 to 10lb leader. Successful patterns include Peter Ross, Black Pennell, Goat's Toe, Invicta and Connemara Black.

Casts should be short with a bushy-top (bob) fly made to trip across the surface to create a disturbance and attract salmon. When a salmon takes a fly, don't strike too quickly. Wait until you feel the weight of the fish on the line before lifting into it.

Lures and Baits

During the spring, salmon rivers often run high due to heavy winter rainfall, possibly supplemented by melting snow up in the headwaters. Even in summer, storms and depressions can raise river water levels significantly. At such times, fly-fishing tends to be ineffective and, so long as the water is not too coloured, spinning is a better option.

While metal lures will readily sink, Devon minnows and plugs will need to be weighted with leads specially designed for the purpose (e.g. a Wye or spiral). Among lures, spinners are notorious for creating line twist, so in addition to the swivel attached to the top of the spinner, tie in another about a foot further up the line.

Devon minnows, in various colour combinations but usually with a yellow belly, are a lure with a long tradition in salmon fishing, while the Toby lure is probably the most famous spoon of all time and has accounted for thousands of salmon. In recent times, the Flying Condom spinner has enjoyed huge success with salmon both in Ireland, where it originated, and in UK waters. It incorporates a revolving blade at its head, while the stem below is long and covered in a thin rubber sheath. Below this is a treble hook. Lures are normally cast across a river and retrieved as they sink, and swing downstream in the flow. How deep they are allowed to sink and how fast they are retrieved will depend on the depth and speed of the water being fished.

Use a spinning rod of around 10ft with a casting capacity of 2oz and combine it with a fixed-spool reel or multiplier reel loaded with a 15 to 20lb line.

When rivers are high and coloured, salmon are often fished for with worms (on size 6 to 8 hooks). Worms are most often legered but sometimes fished below a float.

BELOW Although fly-fishing is the preferred choice of many salmon anglers, during periods of high and low water, lures and baits will often prove more effective.

ABOVE *Prawns can either be deadly for salmon or terrify them, and consequently they are not permitted on many waters.*

With both the leger and float methods the worms are slowly kept on the move across the river bed to attract salmon.

Shrimps and prawns are extreme baits in that they can either be overwhelmingly successful for salmon or cause them to bolt in panic, making other methods tried subsequently totally ineffective. For this reason they are banned on most salmon fisheries. In those waters where they are allowed, they are fished under a float or legered.

All baits for salmon are best fished on a powerful float rod, 12 to 13ft in length, combined with a fixed-spool reel holding 10 to 15lb line.

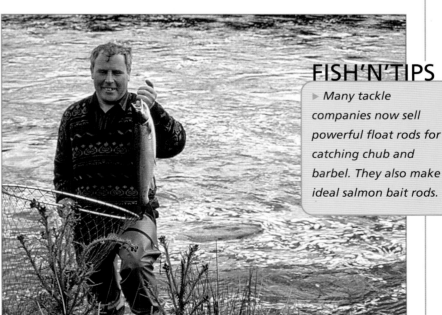

FISH'N'TIPS

▶ *Many tackle companies now sell powerful float rods for catching chub and barbel. They also make ideal salmon bait rods.*

ABOVE *On a river in full spate following heavy rain, a lure or worm are the most likely baits to produce a salmon.*

145

Sea Trout Fishing Methods

Fly-fishing on Rivers

During dry spells in summer, spate rivers will run low and clear, and any sea trout that have run upstream will become wary and hide away during the day in deeper pools that afford them cover (e.g. undercut banks and overhanging trees). After dark they become much more active, splashing and often leaping clear of the water, with some moving further upriver. It is at this time that they can be caught.

Warm and cloudy moonless nights tend to be the most productive time, since sea trout seem to show an aversion to bright moonlight and cold, clear nights.

During the hours of daylight it is a good idea to have a close look at any pools that have not been fished before, but actual fishing should not begin until it is fully dark. To start earlier will disturb any sea trout in the pools and seriously jeopardise the chances of catching any fish that night.

When fishing a venue for the first time it can be worthwhile to go with a friend and fish adjacent pools. If wading, use a staff for support and wear a lifejacket.

Normal tactics are to fish with one, two or even three small wet flies on a floating line; an exciting method to try when fish are active is to strip a floating lure across the pool. This often catches larger than average sea trout, which hammer into the lure as it creates a wake across the surface. If no bites are forthcoming using floating line tactics, it can pay to try fishing a large lure like a Medicine Fly on a sunk line. This tactic often pays off after midnight when any earlier surface activity has quietened down.

Depending on the size of the river being fished, use a rod between 9½ft and 10½ft, matched with a number 6 or 7 line. Use a leader with a breaking strain of at least 8lb to 10lb: sea trout fight incredibly hard

BELOW Sea trout can sometimes be tempted to take a small dry fly during the hours of daylight.

ABOVE *A good night's work. Sea trout are at their most active after dark, particularly on warm, cloudy and moonless nights.*

and the pools in which they hold up are often rocky. On some rivers, particularly in west Wales, sea trout of weights well into double figures are not uncommon.

Sea trout can in some circumstances be caught during the day. On the lower River Test in Hampshire, the short line and heavy nymph tactics devised for grayling have also proved to be successful for sea trout.

ABOVE *Pioneering fly fishermen in the UK and Ireland have shown that sea trout can be caught from river estuaries in daylight.*

In recent years in Ireland, it has begun to be possible to catch sea trout on wet flies in daylight from the estuary of the River Moy. In such a situation, fishing takes place from a drifting boat as it would on a lake.

FISH'N'TIPS

▶ Look for bow waves across the shallows, indicating sea trout are moving upstream and will probably rest in the pool above.

▶ When night fishing, take a torch fitted with new batteries.

▶ After dark, wear clear lens safety glasses to protect your eyes.

Lake Fishing for Sea Trout

Lake fishing for sea trout takes place primarily in Scotland and the west of Ireland. In lakes, sea trout like to lie off rocky promontories and close to islands and reefs, but sometimes shoals will be encountered out in comparatively open water.

The most popular method is to drift in a boat, positioned side-on to the wind, and cast a team of small wet flies – normally three, sometimes four – a short distance ahead before retrieving them.

The top fly in the team is usually bushy, danced across the surface to create a disturbance or wake to attract sea trout.

Normally a floating line is used, though in very windy conditions an intermediate is better

RIGHT Sea trout colour up on returning to fresh water and can become hard to distinguish from any resident brown trout.

BELOW Playing a good sea trout, hooked on a bushy wet fly fished on the top dropper.

as it prevents the flies being whipped across the surface. Alternatively, a fly tied on a double hook can be attached to the point (end) of the leader to act as an anchor.

A rod of 10½ or 11ft, rated for a number 6 or 7 line, will enable the top (bob) fly to be worked effectively across the waves or ripple. Leader strength should be 8 to 10lb.

Successful sea trout wet fly patterns include: Black Pennell, Butcher, Mallard and Claret, Dunkeld and Teal, Blue and Silver. The Red Daddy Longlegs is an excellent bob fly pattern. Use size 10 and 12 flies on windy days, but go as small as a 14 in a light ripple.

An alternative, and less physically demanding, tactic on windy days is to dap. When dapping, a bushy fly is slowly skated

ABOVE Presentation suffers in flat calm conditions, but persevere and there is always the chance of a fish. Small dark dry flies can be effective at such times.

back and forth across the surface by a long (14ft) rod gently moved from side to side and held up at an angle of about 45 degrees.

Use a centrepin or fly reel loaded with about 100 yards of backing line and to the front end tie on 15ft of floss – a lightweight material that catches the wind and carries the fly out over the water. Fish the dapped fly on a short 4ft leader of 6 to 8lb. In really windy conditions, use two flies because the point fly will act as an anchor.

Don't strike too soon when a fish appears at the fly. Let the fish take it and turn away first – it might even be a salmon!

FISH'N'TIPS

▶ *In windy conditions when wet fly fishing, shorten the leader by removing a fly from the team.*

▶ *Use a telescopic dapping rod as it can be retracted and tucked away when not in use.*

149

Lures and Baits

When rivers are running high and coloured after heavy rain, lightly legered lobworms can prove very effective for sea trout. Try fishing a worm on a lead that just fails to hold bottom, and search for sea trout sheltering in slacker water on the edge of the racing current.

As the river begins to fall and clear, spinning becomes a better tactic. Try a small spinner, such as a Mepp, retrieving it as it swings round in the flow from a cast made across the river. For both worming and spinning, use a 10 ft spinning rod and 8lb to 10lb line.

Unlike salmon, sea trout never travel far from their home river when at sea and spend much more of their time feeding close inshore. They are to be found around

RIGHT A magnificent sea trout caught on a Toby lure from a small river that was clearing after a heavy flood.

BELOW An angler struggles to beach a battling sea trout that took a small spinner. Sea trout freshly returned from salt water fight with tremendous power and speed.

ABOVE *Small spinners, such as the Mepp, are very effective for sea trout on rivers that are running high but clearing.*

ABOVE *Sand eels make up a large part of a sea trout's diet when in salt water and are an effective bait in estuaries.*

much of the British Isles coastline and are particularly common along the western shores of Scotland and Ireland. However, for reasons given in the section on sea trout, avoid areas where salmon farms are sited.

On sandy coasts, river estuaries are often wide and shallow and their waters warm rapidly from the spring onwards, providing ideal growing conditions for fry of a variety of species as well as sand eels, which can also be found in such places during the summer months. The presence of all these fish is frequently revealed by diving terns, and sea trout will also often be present to share in the bounty.

Blast-frozen sand eels can be legered or retrieved erratically across the sandy bed to simulate a sickly or injured fish. Live sand eels, if available, are even more effective and can be legered or fished below a float. Look for pools along the river's course, scoured out by the tide or floodwater, as shoals of sea trout will hold in the deeper water.

Rocky river estuaries, and rocky coastlines extending beyond them, can provide excellent sport when spinning with metal lures or plugs for sea trout. Look for spots with clear, deeper water close to the shore and be aware of any seaweed, particularly snaggy bladder wrack, growing out from the rocks. These sea trout are in peak condition, will battle with incredible strength, and often dive into the marginal weed in a last-ditch attempt to shed the hook.

For both beach and rock marks, use a spinning rod of at least 10ft, a reel loaded with 10lb line, and for heavily weeded areas carry a long-handled landing net.

FISH'N'TIPS

▶ *Float-fished maggots can be very effective for sea trout.*

Wild Brown Trout in Stillwaters

Many lakes across northern counties of England, Wales, Scotland and Ireland contain healthy populations of wild brown trout. Lakes lying over limestone bedrock are rich in life, the trout in them thick-set and vividly marked, with heavily spotted golden flanks. Trout here average between 1 and 2lb but can grow much larger, whereas trout from dark, peat-stained and nutrient-poor waters tend to remain small, weighing between 2oz and 8oz at most, and are darkly coloured to match their environment.

These stillwaters are sometimes vast, and the traditional method is known as loch-style fishing, involving casting a team of three, or sometimes four, wet flies from a drifting boat. The tackle and tactics used for loch-style fishing for wild brown trout are the same as for sea trout; however, when trying for brown trout the fly patterns used will change over the course of the season, to reflect the different creatures on which the brown trout will naturally feed. Sea trout wet fly patterns are all designed to trigger an aggressive feeding response.

BELOW The lakes in the Snowdonia National Park in Wales hold excellent stocks of brown trout.

BELOW Two brown trout from the same lake but different locations, clearly showing how their coloration is dictated by environment.

A suitable loch-style leader for both brown trout and sea trout fishing should be made up from 5 to 7lb line and measure around 12ft in length. Make the length of the leader 5ft from the fly line to the top dropper, then allow 3½ft between the two droppers and another 3½ft from the lower dropper to the end (point) of the leader. The droppers are short lengths of a similar breaking strain line, attached to the main leader with a four-turn water knot or tiny dropper rings available from most tackle shops. The droppers should be 6 to 9 inches in length.

The most productive water over which to drift ranges between 2ft and 8ft in depth. It is in these shallow areas that most of a lake's life forms (and food) are concentrated. While brown trout are not a shoal species, they are opportunistic and will gravitate to

ABOVE An early-season brown trout, in tip-top condition, that had been feeding right at the bottom on shrimps and freshwater louse.

Zulu

Black Pennell

Kate McLaren

Peter Ross

Daddy Longlegs

Bibio

Dunkeld

FLIES FOR BROWN TROUT

Effective lake wet fly patterns for wild brown trout include:

Spring	Summer	Autumn
Black Pennell	Invicta	Cinnamon and Gold
Zulu	Dunkeld	Mallard and Claret
Bibio	Green Peter	Silver Invicta
Sooty Olive	Kate McLaren	Peter Ross
Golden Olive Bumble	Dabblers	Daddy Longlegs
Gosling		

ABOVE A light wind ripples the surface as evening closes in. Sedges will begin hatching at this time and a dry sedge imitation will often work.

ABOVE By fishing on the drift, large areas of a lake can be covered in the search for trout.

ABOVE The brown trout of Lough Carra resemble sea trout with their light colouring mirroring the lake's pale marl bed.

any available food source. Plan to drift close in along the shore, around islands and reefs and across any extensive offshore shallows and rocky plateaux.

Fly choice will be dictated by what food items are present in any given lake.

From the spring onwards, when trout often move higher in the water in search of food, the wet fly leader can be used to present a team of dry flies. On many natural trout lakes, hatches of olives and mayflies will occur from April to June, and dry fly imitations will often account for a larger average size of fish than wet flies.

Apply floatant to dry flies to ensure they will ride the waves like a natural insect, but sparingly, as fish are put off by an oily slick emanating from a fly. Degrease the leader also to make it sink, and to be less visible to any fish attracted to the flies.

On many lakes an important part of the trout's diet is made up of small chironomids (midges), which are eaten at all stages of their life cycle. There are many different species and colours, but to anglers they are collectively known as buzzers. In recent years the use of buzzer imitations has become increasingly popular on wild brown trout fisheries, especially in Ireland. On loughs such as Corrib and Mask, excellent catches are now being made on buzzer patterns – often epoxy flies imitating the ascending pupa – fished as a team and either retrieved very slowly or fished statically from a boat.

Dapping is a popular method on both Scottish and Irish lakes (for dapping tackle, see "Lake Fishing for Sea Trout"), though in Ireland it is often practised with natural insects rather than artificials. During late spring mayflies will be used, in high summer grasshoppers, and during late August into September, crane flies (daddy longlegs).

Today, however, many anglers are either too busy or aren't prepared to spend time collecting a supply of bait prior to fishing, and instead buy live insects from pet shops. These include crickets and locusts, sold for feeding to a variety of exotic pets, which, despite not being indigenous to Ireland, are still taken avidly by the trout.

Many large lakes in Scotland and Ireland contain a strain of trout that has evolved solely to eat small fish. Known as ferox, these thrive on a diet of char, perch, smaller trout and any other species present in quantity.

Ferox normally inhabit the deepest parts of a lake and can be caught with large plugs and spoons or dead fish trolled just off bottom.

Ferox are slow growing, live for many years and can grow extremely large. Specimens have been recorded to nearly 30 lb. In Ireland, anglers are now encouraged to return ferox as their numbers have declined significantly in recent years.

FISH'N'TIPS

▶ *Wild brown trout are under increased pressure these days from anglers and the environment, so please return all those caught.*

LEFT A golden late-September brown trout that fell to a small Cinnamon and Gold fished on the point of a team of wet flies.

BELOW A nice brown trout in the net, and perfect wet fly conditions: a good wave and an overcast sky.

Brown and Rainbow Trout in Rivers

Trout rivers can be roughly divided into two basic types: chalkstreams and rain-fed rivers. Chalkstreams emanate from springs in the chalk bedrock and are restricted to the southern counties of England, parts of East Anglia, Derbyshire and Yorkshire. While most contain populations of wild brown trout, intense fishing pressure means that they also have to be stocked, and on most, rainbow trout are introduced as well as farmed brown trout.

Chalkstreams are environments rich in aquatic life and see good hatches of a variety of insects, including olives and mayfly. These form an important part of the trout's diet both as nymphs and adult insects.

Fishing is usually restricted to dry fly until 1 July (when the mayfly season has finished); from this date nymph (the stage in the life of an aquatic insect prior to it hatching out as an adult) fishing is also permitted.

Rain-fed rivers are found throughout Scotland and Wales as well as the north and south west of England. As the name suggests, their daily water level is dictated by rain – or the lack of it. They tend to flow over harder rocks such as granite and through much more rugged landscapes, resulting in the water being far less nutrient-rich, providing trout with poorer feeding opportunities. Many contain only wild stocks of small brown trout, although in areas where fishing pressure is greater they are stocked with fish, mainly brown trout.

Dry flies are fished singly and are always cast upstream. The line is retrieved as the fly drifts back downstream to ensure a fairly tight line between the rod tip and fly, for effective striking when a fish rises. Select a fly to match whatever insects are hatching and cast the fly to land gently a short distance above the rising trout. Try to avoid any of the fly line landing

BELOW While often containing healthy populations of brown trout, rain-fed rivers provide poorer feeding than chalkstreams, resulting in the fish not growing as large.

LEFT By moving stealthily upstream it is possible to wade very close to trout, which can then be covered with a short cast, making less risk of snagging the fly in surrounding vegetation.

pattern when no fish are rising, and account for many landed trout.

Nymph fishing also involves fishing upstream, most commonly with only one fly, although sometimes two are used. Polarising sunglasses will enable trout to be spotted in clear rivers, and even if trout are not actively feeding on nymphs, they can still sometimes be induced to take a fly.

LEFT Netting a plump chalkstream brown trout taken on a dry Mayfly pattern. As fishing becomes more testing after the mayfly season, nymph fishing is also permitted.

above the trout as it will scare it and discourage it from feeding. If you are unsure of the distance between you and a rising trout, try casting the line along the bank parallel with the river first, to get the length right. That way, you avoid spooking any fish. Use a leader slightly shorter than the rod and treat it to make it sink, then treat the dry fly with a floatant.

Two dry fly patterns, the Elk Hair Caddis and the Klinkhammer, designed to imitate hatching sedges, are excellent choices of

LEFT Playing a wild brown trout on a chalkstream carrier. Fishing pressure on chalkstreams necessitates wild trout stocks being supplemented by farmed fish.

Again, the cast should be made a short way upstream of the trout, and as the nymph passes by the trout's nose, the rod tip should be smartly lifted. This causes the nymph to rise, and many trout will take the nymph at this point believing it is trying to escape. Where trout cannot be seen, cast to places where they are likely to be holding.

In clear water, trout can be seen taking the nymph, but where they are not visible, the end of the fly line (and the top part of the leader if it is floating) should be watched. Takes will be shown by the line stopping, twitching, moving upstream or darting to either side. At any of these indications, strike. Various designs of small indicator are available from tackle shops. They attach to the line and work like a float, clearly showing when a trout has taken the fly.

BELOW A slimline river rainbow. Rainbow trout are stocked in many game rivers but breed naturally in only a handful.

BELOW Casting a long line across a river close to overhanging trees. In summer, trout will readily take creatures that fall from the leaves as well as hatching aquatic insects.

LEFT A fine brown trout is drawn over the landing net. Trout wax fat on the rich feeding provided by chalkstreams.

FISH'N'TIPS

▸ Shop-bought tapered leaders will present dry flies more delicately than parallel monofilament.

▸ When fishing a deep pool on a river, attach a sinking braided or poly leader to the tip of a floating fly line to present a nymph well down.

Effective nymph patterns (tied on hook sizes 10 to 14) include Hare's Ear, Pheasant Tail and Mayfly, but leaded shrimp patterns also work well. Carry a selection of differently weighted flies to enable a variety of depths and current speeds to be fished effectively.

Keep low on the horizon when fishing with nymphs and dry flies, and if bankside vegetation makes casting awkward, try wading, if it is allowed on the fishery. By wading carefully it is possible to get very close to fish, making casting easier. Wear a broad-brimmed hat as well as sunglasses to cut down surface glare.

Wet fly fishing for trout is practised on rain-fed rivers but not chalkstreams, and is more a tactic for the spring before weed growth renders it impractical. It is not necessary for trout to be rising for this method to work. A team of two or three wet flies are cast across the river, and bites can come at any time as the flies swing round and downstream in the current towards the near bank (see the section "Wild Brown Trout" for tying a droppered leader).

The tackle required for river trout fishing is the same as that described in the section "Grayling on Fly".

Reservoir Trout Fishing

Bank Fishing

In the spring, when water temperatures are still low, trout are more likely to be found in deep water, feeding on or close to the reservoir bottom. However, when winters have been exceptionally wet and lake levels are high, trout will move on to flooded, grassy margins to feed on drowned lobworms.

Lure fishing

In normal circumstances it pays to head for areas offering deep water close in, such as reservoir dam walls and anywhere the land slopes steeply into the lake.

Food can be in short supply at this time of year and, instead of imitative patterns, lures are normally preferred to trigger an aggressive response from trout. Fish lures on a 9½ or 10ft rod rated for an 8- to 10-weight line. A fast-sinking line will get the lure down quickly: count it down then retrieve the lure just off bottom, varying the speed. Slower retrieves work better when the water is cold. Use a fly line with a sinking rate that matches the depth of water you are fishing. Fish the lure on a leader with a similar length to the rod and with a breaking strain of 8lb to 10lb. Popular early-season lures

BELOW A trout angler makes use of a rocky promontory, enabling him to cast out to the ripple where trout feed more confidently.

include the Sweeney Todd, Ace of Spades and Viva.

Shooting heads enable a lure to be cast much further than is possible with a full (30 yard) fly line, and are excellent for early-season fishing when trout can be a long way out from the bank. They measure between 10 and 12 yards and are attached to a lightweight, but tangle-resistant, shooting/backing line. Shooting heads are produced commercially, but can also be made from a double taper fly line, cut in half then further shortened from the thicker end.

LEFT A small rainbow caught from a dam wall. Dams give access to deep water close in and are a favoured spot at the beginning of the season.

FISH'N'TIPS

▶ *Always fish from the bank before wading out, as trout may be feeding close in.*

As spring progresses into summer and water temperatures rise, trout become more active and will take food at all depths, making it important to have a range of density of fly lines at this time. Most fly reels come with at least one spare spool, and additional spools can be purchased.

Buzzer Fishing

On reservoirs the principal food item in the trout's diet is chironomids (midges, known as "buzzers" by anglers). In the larval stage ("bloodworm") they live in the bottom silt or mud then transform into pupae, which ascend to the surface where they hatch out as adult midges. Pupae can therefore be found anywhere between the lake's bed and the surface.

When fishing buzzer patterns from the bank, choose areas where the wind is light and the water 10 to 15ft deep for much of the retrieve. Imitations are normally

BELOW Warm weather, an overcast sky and a light crosswind: perfect conditions for fishing a team of buzzers on a floating line, letting them drift slowly round on the ripple.

fished in a team of three, on a floating line and a long (20ft) leader that will present the trio from midwater to the bottom.

Tie up a droppered leader (see "Wild Brown Trout" for constructing droppers) from 6lb to 8lb line, with 10ft of line between the fly line and top dropper, 5ft between the two droppers and 5ft between the lower dropper and the end (point) of the leader. Since it is virtually invisible under water and is also a sinking line, fluorocarbon is the best material to use.

BELOW A deep-bodied stock fish that fell for a black lure. In the early spring, when the water is still cold, fish react more slowly to flies.

LEFT Four stockie rainbows caught at long range using a lure and a sinking shooting head on a breezy spring day.

Takes to slowly retrieved or wind-drifted buzzers tend to be really positive, with the line suddenly shooting tight and the trout taking the hook. When midges can be seen hatching, use lighter buzzer patterns, and retrieve them straight after casting so as to fish them higher in the water.

Modern epoxy buzzer patterns, in green, red and black and on hook sizes 10 to 16, are extremely realistic and highly effective. It pays to have a selection tied up in a variety of shades and on different size hooks, to ensure the natural prey can be matched on any given water, day and even time of day, for there are hundreds of different buzzer varieties!

The heaviest fly should be fished on the point to sink quickly to the bottom. Wait a few seconds before starting the retrieve; this must be as slow as possible to simulate the natural movement of chironomids.

If a light wind is blowing along the shore, it often pays not to retrieve at all and instead allow the surface drift to slowly carry the fly line, leader and buzzers round in an arc.

Dry Fly Fishing

When buzzers are hatching (normally from early morning), try fishing with a team of emerger or dry fly patterns (or a combination) treated with floatant. Adult midges return to the water in the evening to lay eggs on the surface, and can also be imitated with dry flies. Ensure the leader is treated with leader sink.

BELOW Reservoir landing stages provide shelter for fry of many coarse species and, in turn, attract predatory trout.

RIGHT Happiness is trout-shaped! A silvery rainbow seen rising close to the bank, that fell to a carefully presented small dry sedge pattern.

BELOW Boat and bank anglers take advantage of a concentration of trout feeding close in. When newly introduced, rainbow trout often head straight for the downwind shore.

Successful dry fly patterns include Shipman's Buzzer and Bob's Bits – both are commercially tied in a variety of colours.

Nymphs are suggestive patterns that imitate midges as well as a variety of other aquatic creatures, and are fished in a similar way to buzzers. Dry flies, emergers and nymphs are all best fished using a number 6 or 7 float on a $9\frac{1}{2}$ or 10ft rod.

When fishing from the bank, try working flies close to features that are likely to attract trout, such as hedgerows and fences that disappear into the water. These would once have bordered fields that are now drowned, and will attract all manner of aquatic creatures including fry and, to feed on them all, trout.

Falls of land-based insects also regularly occur on reservoirs, and include the hawthorn fly in spring, ants, beetles and ladybirds in summer and crane flies (daddy longlegs) in autumn. Being opportunists, trout will readily rise to these bonus food supplies and it is well worth having some imitative patterns available in the fly box.

LEFT Playing a good fish hooked in a quiet bay on a dry fly. Trout will readily rise to take terrestrial insects blown on to the water.

Many reservoir trout fisheries now allow fish to be returned after capture. However, when retaining fish to eat, dispatch them quickly and humanely with a priest, then use a marrow spoon to inspect their stomach contents. Spooning the first fish of the day to see what it has been eating may confirm your tactics are correct or a fluke and, if the latter, guide you to an alternative and more effective approach.

Wading

To enable bank anglers to cover more water, most reservoirs allow wading. At one time, only thigh waders were permitted, but recently this has been extended to include waist waders. When wading and fishing with any density line, including a floater, it pays to use a line tray. These are attached around the waist and retrieved line is fed into them ready for the next cast. Without a line tray, casting is seriously hampered: floating lines will drift downwind in a breeze and have to be hauled back, while sinking lines will need to be continually pulled up in the water for any casting distance to be attained. Line trays are also very useful when

fishing from rocky and overgrown banks where fly lines will constantly get caught up.

Landing nets are available with a spike incorporated into the bottom of the handle, designed specifically for anglers who like to wade. Pushed into the lake bed, the net is close at hand, and can also be employed as a line tray when angled for retrieved line to be fed into it. They can also be used to gauge the depth when initially wading out.

ABOVE Most reservoirs are stocked with trout weighing between 1lb and 2lb, with a sprinkling of larger fish for added interest.

Boat Fishing

While many of the methods used from a boat are similar to those employed when fishing off the bank, going afloat on a reservoir provides access to the waters in their entirety.

Lure fishing can be effective right through the season, though the depth at which trout will be feed will vary widely, from at bottom early in the season to anywhere between the surface and the lake bed in high summer, making it necessary to have a range of different density fly lines to be able to locate them consistently.

Lures can be fished when drifting or from a static boat. It is worth drifting to search for trout until a shoal is located, then putting the anchor down over the hotspot. Alternatively, the position of the fish can be noted and then repeatedly drifted over. Lures can be fished singly or with a second lure on a dropper 4ft above. The overall leader length should be 12ft.

A boat drifting side-on to the wind will move more slowly than one with its bows pointing downwind, controlled by the rudder. Side-on, the casts are made in front of the boat and the lure pulled straight back. In a boat with bows downwind, casting is out to the side, with the line and a lure allowed to swing round in an arc before being retrieved.

Buoyant Booby patterns catch a lot of trout when fished on a fast-sinking line from an anchored boat. They are twitch-retrieved along the bottom on a short (1 to 3ft) leader, and the only drawback of this pattern is that trout often swallow them, are deep hooked and have to be dispatched.

Lure Fishing

Lure fishing with sinking lines requires a powerful 9 to 10ft rod capable of casting

LEFT An average-sized rainbow nestles at the bottom of a landing net that is far too deep for reservoir trout.

lines of 8 to 10-weight. Effective lure patterns include Whiskey Lure, Appetizer, Cat's Whisker, Black Lure and Church Fry. Fish on hook sizes 6 to 10 with a leader strength of 10lb.

Wet Fly Fishing

Wet fly fishing from a drifting boat has long been a popular and productive method on reservoirs. Trout, particularly rainbows, feed heavily on daphnia, a tiny creature found in rich lowland reservoirs in huge numbers. Daphnia are sensitive to light and on bright days will be at depth, while on gloomy days and

FISH'N'TIPS

▶ A big black lure fished on the point of a wet fly leader often proves deadly at last light.

▶ Wear clear-lens safety glasses rather than sunglasses when watching dry flies in the evening and on dull days.

BELOW A brace of silvery, full-finned rainbows. The quality of trout stocked in most reservoirs is excellent and with rich feeding they show rapid growth.

at dawn and dusk they are close to the surface. Trout swim through clouds of daphnia, mouths open, engulfing huge quantities of food.

If trout are not obviously feeding at the surface, fish a team of wet flies on a succession of fly lines with different densities, and thus sinking rates, to locate them. Vary the speed of the retrieve as well as the depth, and use one or more flies in the team that incorporate orange in their dressing – it is an infallible colour when trout are feeding on daphnia. When the top dropper reaches the surface by the boat at the end of the retrieve, wait for a few seconds before lifting off and re-casting as trout will often follow flies some distance before taking them.

BELOW Grafham Water in Huntingdon, where exceptional trout fishing has been experienced since it opened in the 1960s.

LEFT A hard-fighting rainbow, tempted with a Diawl Bach nymph, is safely netted. During flat calms many anglers fish nymphs below an indicator.

BELOW Freed to fight another day. Many reservoir trout fisheries now allow fish to be returned, and sell special catch-and-release day tickets.

Create a Wake

When trout are feeding close to or at the surface, on daphnia or hatching insects, fish a bushy fly on the top dropper and work it across the surface on the retrieve to create a wake or disturbance that will attract trout. Reservoir rainbows frequently chase wet flies for some yards before biting, and a sizeable bow wave will often be clearly visible behind the fly being hunted down.

Droppered leaders (see "Wild Brown Trout" for their construction) for wet fly fishing on reservoirs should measure around 18ft with 10ft between fly line and top dropper, 4ft between droppers and 4ft between the second (middle) dropper and the end (point) of

LEFT Sitting on a thwart board when drift fishing provides an elevated position from which to cast and watch for rising fish ahead of the boat.

the leader. Construct it from 6 to 8lb line and fish it on a rod 10½ to 11ft long, rated 6/7. Popular reservoir wet fly patterns include Pearly Bodied Wickhams, Bruce's Bug, Oakham Orange, Bibio and Silver Invicta. Fish them on hook sizes 10 to 14, depending on wave height (the bigger the wave, the larger the fly).

When lure or wet fly fishing on windy days, it pays to use a drogue to slow down the speed of a drifting boat. Without one, fishing becomes too rushed, presentation suffers and

FISH'N'TIPS

▶ Walking boots are more comfortable to wear than Wellingtons when out boat fishing in hot weather.

▶ Keep any big fish hooked in front of the boat and well away from anchor or drogue ropes.

▶ Wrap up warm when going out in a boat in cold weather as there is no shelter from the wind.

LEFT Most reservoir brown trout caught during the day fall to lures fished deep where light levels are low.

ABOVE A silvery scaled rainbow trout receives an admiring glance from its captor. During the summer rainbow trout will readily take surface-fished flies, providing great visual excitement.

hotspots or shoals of fish are rapidly passed. Drogues act like a parachute and are attached midway along the rear gunwale on a boat drifting side-on to the wind. They can also be used off the stern when drifting with the bow into the wind on breezy days.

Dry Fly Fishing

Dry flies are very effective on reservoirs from late spring through to the summer, when daily hatches of chironomids occur. Fish with them from a drifting boat on a similar leader length and strength to that used for wet flies, though ultra-fine co-polymer line is a better choice than standard, thicker monofilament. Fluorocarbon is not suitable for small dry flies as it sinks and will pull them under. Degrease the leader and apply a floatant sparingly to the dry flies to help them ride the ripple.

Trout can be caught on dry flies on windy days, but it can prove a frustrating exercise as waves will frequently swamp and drown the flies. For effective striking use a 10ft crisp-actioned rod rated for 6- or 7-weight line. Popular patterns include Hoppers, Bob's Bits and Shipman's Buzzers. Use claret-bodied patterns on dull days and hot orange versions on bright, sunny days.

In late summer and autumn floating fry patterns can prove deadly for trout feeding hard on coarse fish fry. Trout will work along the edge of weedbeds charging into fry hiding there and a floating fry pattern gives the impression of a small, stunned fish. Anchor the boat by a weedbed and intercept trout as they patrol past.

ABOVE *On bright, windless days trout will often go deep, and need to be fished for with sinking lines.*

BELOW *A fine brace of grown-on reservoir rainbows. Trout into double figures are caught from such fisheries every year.*

Buzzer Fishing

Buzzers and nymphs can be fished from a drifting boat so long as the wind is light, since the flies must be retrieved very slowly. Even better is to not move the flies at all and just take in line as the boat drifts

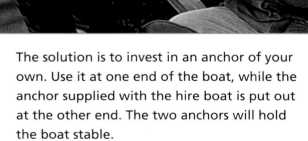

towards them. A popular tactic is to fish the flies under an indicator attached above the top dropper and watch it for bites. Indicators can also be used with buzzers and nymphs from the bank, particularly from dam walls and at concrete bowl reservoirs where the water is deep close to the bank.

Buzzers and nymphs are more commonly fished from an anchored boat, as the flies can be fished far more slowly and under more control. In flat calm conditions they are often fished under an indicator.

On windier days, the boat will swing from side to side when held by one anchor, causing the fly line and leader to repeatedly slacken and tighten, adversely affecting presentation.

The solution is to invest in an anchor of your own. Use it at one end of the boat, while the anchor supplied with the hire boat is put out at the other end. The two anchors will hold the boat stable.

Epoxy buzzers are ideal for reservoir trout and are available in a wide variety of colours. Red, green and black are the most effective. Use in sizes 10 to 14, and try to match any hatch for colour and size. Popular nymphing patterns include the Diawl Bach, Hare's Ear Nymph and Pheasant Tail Nymph. Fish nymphs and buzzers on a fluorocarbon leader 20ft long (10ft–5ft–5ft) with a 6 to 8lb breaking strain. The 10ft rod used for dry fly fishing is also useable for buzzer and nymph fishing.

FISH'N'TIPS

▶ *On hot days, don't hang a bag with trout in it over the side of the boat and in the water – they will "boil". Instead, tuck the bag under a boat seat out of the sun and dampen periodically.*

Small Stillwater Trout Fishing

A definition of a small stillwater trout fishery would be any lake up to around 30 acres in size. There are many such fisheries across the country; some consist of a series of pools rather than one lake and are often stocked with different-sized fish.

Where trout are grown on in cages on site, the fishery will usually be stocked every morning before anglers arrive. Those where the trout have to be brought in by tanker from a fish farm will normally be stocked once or twice per week.

Rainbow Trout

The vast majority of these small stillwater fisheries stock only with rainbow trout, though this may include a proportion of the recently developed and very attractive blue and golden strains. The rainbows will usually average 2 to 3lb, with a scattering of larger fish into double figures, though some fisheries will stock with trout well over 12lb, or even over 20lb, in order to attract anglers.

After they have been introduced, these big rainbows do not grow on and will actually lose weight and condition, since they find it impossible to match the protein-rich diet of pellets consumed in the stew pond. It is therefore very much in the interest of the fishery owner that these fish are caught as soon as possible after their introduction.

BELOW Almost there! An angler requires a helping hand as he applies maximum pressure to bring a battling rainbow trout to the net.

BELOW A deep-bodied rainbow trout typical of those caught from many small stillwater fisheries, having been raised on a diet of high-protein pellets.

Brown Trout

Some fisheries do stock up with brown trout to provide variety, although, being slower-growing, they are much more expensive to rear and their numbers are usually very limited. If they remain at liberty, brown trout can fare quite well in these small environments and actually increase in weight.

During periods of warm weather small stillwater trout can stop biting and become very difficult to catch. Often the introduction of fresh trout stirs up the torpid resident stock and sees both them and the newcomers willing to take a fly.

LEFT *A nicely proportioned rainbow trout tempted out from under the cover of overhanging bushes by the arrival, with an audible plop, of a weighted nymph.*

FISH'N'TIPS

▶ *Introduced trout quickly become wary of anglers. Lakes stocked on a daily basis usually fish better in the morning for this reason.*

▶ *Trout often lie under marginal weedbeds. Lower weighted nymphs into holes in the weedbeds and jiggle them up and down.*

LEFT *An angler struggles to haul his prize ashore. When stalking trout in clearwater fisheries, wear good-quality polarising sunglasses and sombre clothing, and keep below the skyline.*

Stalking

The most exciting way to catch small stillwater trout is to stalk them, and for this you need clear water. Stalking also enables you to be selective and only target the larger fish in a lake. Invest in a good-quality pair of polarising sunglasses and a long-peaked cap or broad-brimmed hat to further reduce glare.

To be successful in stalking it is important to be mobile, so carry only essential items and travel light. A telescopic, folding landing net can be clipped onto a multi-pocketed waistcoat that carries all the small accessories needed. Wear sombre clothing and keep off the skyline – even recently introduced trout can be put off by a clumsy approach.

Rainbow trout will usually be seen patrolling these small stillwaters, while brown trout tend to be territorial and remain in one area for most of the time. Both species will never be far from cover, and can be found close to overhanging trees and bushes and under marginal weed rafts. They are also attracted to inflowing streams because of their cool oxygenated water and food items washed down on the current.

Dry Flies

Most small stillwater trout fall to nymph patterns, but they can be caught on dry flies. A non-specific dry fly can sometimes be the downfall of a wily brown trout that has resisted all the nymphs cast to it, while lakes experiencing good hatches of olives and mayfly will see trout rising to take them.

Larger waters may also see hatches of chironomids and sedges, while falls of terrestrial flies like ants and crane flies (daddy longlegs) will also sometimes bring trout to the surface. If any coarse fish are present, often the trout will also feed on their fry from late summer.

When a patrolling trout is seen, the fly should be cast in front of and beyond it. Most of the nymph patterns used on these waters are leaded to ensure they sink rapidly, for these trout will often only take a fly on the same level at which they are swimming. Once the cast fly

BELOW Many fly patterns used on small stillwaters are weighted to quickly reach the depth of patrolling trout.

BELOW On lakes where hatches of fly occur or terrestrial creatures are regularly blown out on to the water, trout will readily come to the surface to feed on them and can be caught on dry flies.

FISH'N'TIPS

▶ *Fish a Polystickle in the autumn if trout are feeding on fry.*

▶ *Finding two or three trout swimming together greatly increases the chances of a catch, because of the competitive element.*

has sunk to the same depth as the trout, it should be drawn across in front of its nose. Sometimes trout will be attracted by the plop of a weighted fly entering the water and take it on the drop.

Going Afloat

On larger fisheries and those where the water is coloured, stalking is not really an option. However, maintain the mobile approach and work your way round the bank, casting half a dozen times or so in each spot. On some bigger lakes a boat is available; this will enable fish to be targeted that are out of reach of bank anglers or that have gone deep right in the middle of the lake during a prolonged spell of bright, hot weather.

Successful nymph patterns include: Montana, Hare's Ear, Prince, Damsel and Walker's Mayfly. These should be fished on a 5 to 7lb fluorocarbon leader slightly shorter than the rod, 9ft or 9½ ft with a 5- or 6-weight floating line.

ABOVE *If not caught soon after being stocked, huge rainbows begin to lose weight and condition.*

ABOVE *A handsome brace of rainbows also shows the variation in colour that can occur.*

ABOVE *On waters where trout cannot be seen, adopt a mobile approach, pausing to cast five or six times in each spot.*

Grayling Fishing
Grayling on Fly

As most grayling live in waters preserved for the major game species, fishing for them doesn't usually start until the autumn, when the close season for trout and salmon begins.

Grayling will take food from the surface down to the riverbed, enabling a variety of fly-fishing methods to be used to catch them. Much of the tackle, and some of the tactics, required to catch grayling on the fly are similar to those used for river trout and are covered in more detail earlier in the book.

Dry Flies

BELOW Grayling thrive in cold and unpolluted streams and rivers, and in the UK are at the southern limit of their range.

Even into autumn, weed growth can still be prolific on many rivers and this often makes the dry fly the most effective tactic. It is best to match the artificial fly used to any flies seen hatching, but because of the competitive element

seen in shoal species like grayling, this is not always essential. Tried and tested patterns include the Red Tag, plus various olives and sedges tied on size 10 to 16 hooks.

Wet Flies

Grayling can be caught on dry flies during the winter, for even on the coldest days hatches of insects will occur. However, during the winter, fishing with wet flies or nymphs is the more usual method. Popular wet fly patterns include

BELOW Grayling can be caught on a wide variety of fly patterns throughout the season, though the use of heavily weighted nymphs has become extremely popular in recent years.

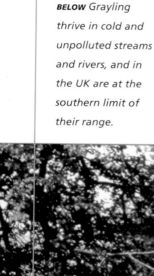

LEFT On clearwater fisheries, avoid spooking grayling by keeping low and fishing upstream. Grayling will often rise to a dry fly even when no natural insects are hatching.

FISH'N'TIPS

▶ *Pink-coloured shrimps are effective for grayling.*

▶ *Take the occasional grayling for the table; they are excellent for eating.*

LEFT Fishing a leaded nymph into the deep water of a chalkstream hatch pool, where big grayling often lie on the edge of the fast water.

the Red Tag, Coachman and Alder on size 12 and 14 hooks. Winter nymph fishing for grayling has become increasingly popular in recent decades, since eastern European anglers began revealing their alternative short line tactics, with heavily weighted nymphs that can prove devastatingly effective.

Nymphs

To present these patterns most effectively it is usually necessary to wade, and by approaching a glide slowly and carefully it is possible to get very close to the grayling holding station there. Very short casts are made upstream and the heavy nymphs worked back downstream along the bottom, so that they look exactly like an aquatic creature being washed down on the current. The nymphs are either fished under an indicator or the line is watched for bites.

Whether fishing dry flies, wet flies or nymphs, adopt a mobile approach. A shoal of grayling will quickly become agitated when several of their number have been caught, so move on in search of other groups, which will also make for more interesting fishing. Wear polarising sunglasses to spot fish and wade if possible, allowing you to get closer to the fish, making casting easier.

RECOMMENDED TACKLE

Method	Venue	Rod	Fly line (All floating)
Dry fly	Small streams	7–8ft	3–4 weight DT line
Dry fly	Rivers	9–9½ft	4–5 weight DT line
Wet fly	Rivers	9–9½ft	4–5 weight DT line
Nymph	Rivers	10–10½ft	4–5 weight DT line

Leader material: Tapered leaders in standard monofilament with 2lb point or 4lb BS co-polymer low-stretch line.

Grayling on Bait

When water temperatures plummet, most species switch off from feeding and become far less active. Grayling, however, are very much the exception: being a cold-water species, they will feed hard even after the heaviest overnight frosts.

Adopt a Roving Approach

Trotting for grayling on a crisp and sunny winter's day is hugely enjoyable. Travelling light will encourage you to explore a fishery rather than just sit in one spot. Bait fishing for grayling is all about roaming and searching a stream or river, catching a few fish from a glide then moving on in search of another shoal. As well as being a more interesting style of fishing, roving keeps the circulation going at a time when temperatures may not rise much above freezing all day.

BELOW There are few more pleasant ways to spend a crisp winter's day than trotting for grayling. Regularly moving to a fresh swim keeps the fishing interesting.

Wear a waistcoat for holding all the small items necessary for a day's trotting and a pouch round the waist for holding the bait.

A folding landing net can be clipped on to a waist belt or the waistcoat itself, leaving just the rod to be carried by hand. Fish by standing, kneeling or sitting on the bank.

A 13ft trotting rod with a waggler-style middle-to-tip action is best, for not only will it enable bites at up to 40 yards, but the more

BELOW A fine brace of grayling taken on an ideal trotting outfit consisting of a lightweight float rod, centrepin reel and a broad-topped buoyant float.

LEFT Play big grayling that were hooked in heavy water carefully, to prevent the hook pulling out.

FISH'N'TIPS

▶ After catching several grayling from a glide on maggots, try trotting a whole lobworm. The tactic often produces a really big fish.

▶ The only conditions grayling don't like are high, coloured water.

forgiving tip will ensure that the hook does not pull out if a bigger grayling begins to lunge on a short line in the fast current. Choose a slim, lightweight rod that will be comfortable to hold all day.

A centrepin should be the reel of choice, since it ensures constant direct contact with the float for more sensitivity, allowing bigger fish to be played.

Buoyant, broad-topped floats such as Chubbers and Loafers are best for carrying a bait in the fast glides where grayling live. The float should be held back gently so that the bait precedes the float down the flow.

Hooks and Baits

Use line strengths of $2^{1}/_{2}$ to 3lb, with single maggots fished on size 16 to 18 hooks, and double or treble maggots on 12s or 14s. Sweetcorn, an excellent grayling bait, should be presented on size 10 or 12 hooks, and worms on anything between an 8 and a 14 depending on their size. Introduce samples of the hookbait with every cast, but use them sparingly to avoid overfeeding a shoal.

Check the hookpoint regularly, as tripping baits over gravelly bottoms will see hooks become blunt, as will catching and unhooking a succession of bony-mouthed grayling.

ABOVE Unlike most species, grayling will feed well on bitterly cold days.

RIGHT During winter grayling will form big shoals, and by regularly feeding a swim large numbers can be caught. Maggots, sweetcorn and small red worms are all excellent baits.

SEA FISHING

For many the great attraction of sea fishing is the total freedom that it offers, often against a backdrop of spectacular scenery. In sea fishing there are no permits or licences to buy, no restrictions on when and where you can fish and no limit on the number of fish (bass excepted) that can be taken for the table.

Despite the pressures of commercial fishing, the waters around the British Isles still hold a multitude of species

MAIN PICTURE Fly-fishing the surf for bass. When the sea clears after storms, bass will move close inshore in search of food washed from the sand.

and, as a result of global warming and the rise in sea temperatures, they are now being joined by a procession of southern European species migrating north. Species like the trigger fish, gilt head and couch's bream are now regular captures along the southern coasts of Britain and Ireland, and are sure not to stop there. Bass, too, are also spreading north as waters warm up with fish now regularly reported from Northern Ireland, Scotland and even further north in Norway!

In sea angling, big fish frequently turn up totally unexpectedly; often, when a rod hoops over as a fish bites, the angler will have no idea for a time just what they have hooked. With the arrival of new species to home waters, the unpredictability and excitement of the sport are sure to increase even further.

While sea fishing can be neatly divided into two basic categories of boat and shore, there are many different aspects to both. Shore fishing encompasses storm and open beaches, estuaries, piers and harbours and rocky coastlines, and going afloat can entail fishing inshore from a small dinghy or venturing many miles out in a charter boat to fish over sandbanks, wrecks and reefs.

Although the methods used at different locations may be similar, the species present vary and will also frequently change during the course of the year. Over time, the progressive sea angler will learn about the right tackle, tactics and baits that need to be used at a range of venues for fish to be caught consistently.

A wide variety of appropriate baits can be bought from coastal tackle shops, though many are also available for free to the angler who is prepared to spend time collecting them. Gathering bait will also bring an appreciation of the tides, and understand how they affect different locations and the species that live there.

Sea fishing is a constant challenge, with rarely two days' fishing alike, which makes it all the more fascinating!

BELOW A day out boat fishing can see a range of setups used to catch a variety of species.

BELOW LEFT Safely landed. A charter boat skipper prepares to unhook a pirk-caught cod taken many miles offshore over rough ground.

BELOW RIGHT Bass are a highly prized species that can be caught from many boat marks and shore locations on both natural and artificial baits.

Sea-Fishing Species
Bass

BELOW Bass are active hunters and are often caught on lures as well as with legered baits.

Dicenthracus labrax

IDENTIFICATION

Bass are striking in appearance, with metallic blue/green backs and shimmering silver flanks. Their undersides are white and the fins light grey. Dorsal and anal fins and gill covers are all edged with sharp spines. Smaller fish are known as school bass.

LOCATION/HABITAT

Although the bass's range is increasing (it is now found as far north as Scotland), the largest populations are much further south along the south, south-east and south-west coasts of Britain and Ireland.

As the sea warms from late spring, bass begin to move inshore to feed. They can be found along rocky coastlines, over sand and shingle beaches, and in river estuaries where they often move up into freshwater in search of food.

DIET/BAIT

Bass are active hunters and include sand eels, sprats, mackerel, crabs, prawns and squid in their diet. After rough weather they will move close to the water's edge on beaches in search of worms and shellfish dislodged from the sand. Razorfish, clams and lugworm can be very effective baits at this time. During the winter, a mackerel head fished after dark in the surf can pick up lone specimen bass.

British Records
Shore: 19lb.   Boat: 19lb 9oz 2dr.

Cod
Gadus Morhua

BELOW In summer, cod are found offshore over deep-water wrecks and reefs.

IDENTIFICATION

Cod are scavengers, with large heads and huge mouths lined with small teeth, while the body is round and deep bellied, clearly not designed for speed. Colouring on the back and sides varies from olive grey through to brown, with significant mottling on the flanks. The upper jaw protrudes and there is a single barbel under the chin. Cod are a shoal species. Fish below 5 to 6lb are known as codling.

LOCATION/HABITAT

In Scotland, cod are present around the coast all year round, but further south they move offshore during the summer to deep water over rough ground and wrecks. From the autumn onwards, many migrate towards the coast to feed over rocky, stony and sandy beaches at high tide.

DIET/BAIT

Cod primarily feed on the bottom on worms, small flatfish, pouting, crabs and prawns, but will also take herring and sprats in midwater. Cod over wrecks and reefs are often caught on big artificial eels and pirks. Inshore, lugworm and squid baits will do the trick.

British Records
Shore: 44lb 8oz.   Boat: 58lb 6oz.

Whiting
Merlangius merlangus

IDENTIFICATION
The whiting's body is streamlined, with silvery flanks. The back is a darker grey-brown with a hint of pink. The whiting's mouth is full of small, sharp teeth.

LOCATION/HABITAT
Large shoals of whiting migrate inshore from late summer and are then common all around the coasts of the UK and Ireland during the winter. They prefer sand and shingle seabeds and will move into very shallow water to feed.

DIET/BAIT
Like their close relative the cod, whiting are predatory and feed mainly on small fish near the seabed. They can be caught on lugworm, mackerel and squid strip.

British Records

Shore: 4lb 0oz 7dr.   Boat: 6lb 12oz.

LEFT Although boat anglers will catch whiting during the day, fishing for them from the shore is normally more productive at night.

Pouting
Gadus luscus

IDENTIFICATION
Pouting or bib have short squat bodies and golden-brown backs. The flanks are lighter and sport dark vertical stripes. There is a black spot on the pectoral fins and a barbel under the chin.

LOCATION/HABITAT
Resident all around the UK, adult pouting prefer deeper water over rough ground, while younger fish often swarm inshore on beaches and around piers and breakwaters.

DIET/BAIT
Shrimps, worms, molluscs. Small pouting are often used as bait for cod, bass and conger eels.

British Records

Shore: 4lb 9oz.   Boat: 5lb 8oz.

LEFT Most pouting caught from the shore are small, but make effective baits for predatory species such as cod and bass.

FISH'N'TIPS
▶ *Fish after dark for hectic sport with both whiting and pouting.*

183

Mullet

All three species of mullet that occur around the British Isles live on a diet of algae and minute food items (diatoms) hoovered up from the bottom mud.

During summer, shoals of all three species can be found in estuaries, harbours and marinas. They are all very similar in appearance, with flat, blunt heads, spiked dorsal fins, and bodies covered in large scales. Although they lead sedate lives, all are ferocious fighters when hooked.

Thick-Lipped Mullet
Chelon labrosus

BELOW Thick-lipped mullet can be weaned off their natural diet by groundbaiting with mashed bread or fish, then caught on flake or fish strip.

Thick-lipped mullet can be weaned off their natural diet by groundbaiting with mashed bread or fish and then float fishing flake or fish strip hookbaits. Thick-lipped mullet will travel long distances up rivers.

British Records
Shore: 14lb 2oz 12dr.   Boat: 10lb 1oz.

Thin-Lipped Mullet
Liza ramada

Thin-lipped mullet are easier to catch than thick-lips, the best tactic being a small spinner with a segment of ragworm impaled on the points of the rear treble hook. Thin-lipped mullet will also move into freshwater in search of food.

British Records
Shore: 7lb.   Boat: 5lb 15oz.

Golden Grey Mullet
Liza aurata

Slimmer than other mullet, with a distinctive gold spot above each gill cover, golden greys rarely venture into freshwater and are as likely to be found in harbours as in open water off beaches. Small worm baits and strips of mackerel work well.

British Records
Shore: 3lb 8oz 8dr.   Boat: 2lb 13oz 6dr.

Coalfish and Pollack

Coalfish and pollack are closely related members of the cod family and are very similar in appearance.

Coalfish
Pollachius virens

IDENTIFICATION

Coalfish inhabiting deep water are dark grey-green in colour, while those from shallow areas exhibit brighter, more olive-brown tones. Their bodies are smooth and muscular. Both the belly and lateral line are creamy white.

LOCATION/HABITAT

Coalfish are widely distributed throughout the British Isles, though they are more populous in the north, where they are also known as coleys and saithe. Bigger fish inhabit the deeps over rough ground, whereas smaller fish live inshore off rocky coastlines and around harbours.

DIET/BAIT

Sand eels, mackerel, herring.

British Records

Shore: 24lb 11oz 12dr.   Boat: 37lb 5oz.

Pollack
Pollachius pollachius

IDENTIFICATION

The metallic green-brown flanks of pollack are overlaid with a dark lateral line. Unlike on coalfish, the lower jaw is prominent.

LOCATION/HABITAT

Pollock are all around Britain and Ireland, over wrecks and reefs and close to rocky shorelines. Bigger fish tend to be out in deep water, and in the largest populations in the west and south-west.

DIET/BAIT

Small fish (rockling, wrasse, blennies), crabs and sand eels. Silvery feathers and bar spoons are effective off rocks.

British Records

Shore: 18lb 4oz.   Boat: 29lb 4oz.

FISH'N'TIPS

▶ *Big artificial eels catch many big coalfish and pollack over wrecks.*

ABOVE *Small coalfish live close in along rocky coastlines, while larger fish prefer to inhabit offshore rough ground in deep water.*

ABOVE *Pollack are very common along rocky coasts, although the biggest specimens come from deep-water reefs and wreck marks.*

Haddock, Ling and Hake

Haddock and ling are both members of the cod family, live in large shoals and sport barbels under their chins.

FISH'N'TIPS

▶ Big ling are caught out from West Country ports.

Haddock
Melanogrammus aeglefinus

IDENTIFICATION

The haddock's back is dark green or brown. The flanks with their silvery sheen progressively lighten down to a white belly. The head is small and the eyes large. The black lateral line is prominent and there is a dark spot above each pectoral fin.

LOCATION/HABITAT

Most common off the west coast of Scotland and Ireland. Haddock live in deep water over rough or broken ground.

DIET/BAIT

A bottom feeder mainly eating shellfish, worms, starfish and crabs. Occasionally fish. Squid strip is effective.

British Records

Shore: 6lb 12oz.   Boat: 13lb 11oz 4dr.

Ling
Molva molva

IDENTIFICATION

Ling possess eel-like bodies with a mottled grey-brown colouring.

LOCATION/HABITAT

Resident all around the British Isles. Ling live in deep water favouring rocky ground, reefs and wrecks. Occasionally caught off cliff marks.

DIET/BAIT

Any small fish. Ling most often take baited pirks.

British Records

Shore: 21lb 10oz.   Boat: 59lb 8oz.

Hake
Merluccius merluccius

Hake are similar in appearance to ling and share the same habitat but are only caught regularly off southern Ireland.

British Records

Shore: 3 lb 8 oz 2 dr.   Boat: 25 lb 12 oz 14 dr.

FISH'N'TIPS

▶ A section of freshwater eel is a top bait for tope.

ABOVE Tope hunt over clean ground and in strong currents and many are caught from boats fishing in large estuaries.

Tope
Galeorhinus galeus

IDENTIFICATION

Tope are a member of the shark family. Their sleek bodies are grey-brown along the back and flanks, gradually lightening to a white underside. The fins are large and powerful and can generate great speed. The teeth are sharp and triangular.

LOCATION/HABITAT

All around the British Isles during summer, with notable areas including the Thames and Shannon estuaries and Strangford Lough. Tope prefer clean ground and strong currents and will hunt anywhere from midwater to the bottom. Most are caught from boats.

DIET/BAIT

Any small fish, including pouting, whiting, mackerel, and flatfish.

British Records

Shore: 66lb.   Boat: 82lb 8oz.

Spurdog
Squalus acanthias

IDENTIFICATION

Spurdog can be told apart from other dogfish by the sharp spines at the leading edge of each dorsal fin and the absence of an anal fin. Spurdog are long and slim, with a grey back and flanks that graduate to a white belly. They possess razor-sharp teeth for slicing through their prey.

LOCATION/HABITAT

Present throughout UK and Irish waters but especially in Wales and along the west coast

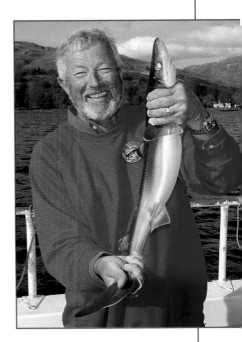

RIGHT *Spurdog can be easily identified by the sharp spine at the front of each dorsal fin.*

of Scotland. They are mostly caught by boat anglers between spring and autumn.

DIET/BAIT

Spurdog feed on any small fish encountered while hunting in shoals at midwater.

British Records
Shore: 16lb 12oz 8dr.
Boat: 21lb 3oz 7dr.

Lesser-Spotted Dogfish
Scyllium canicula

IDENTIFICATION

Lesser-spotted dogfish have exceedingly coarse skin varying from grey-brown to orange-brown on the back and flanks, overlaid with numerous small dark spots. The mouth is underslung and filled with sharp teeth. Their eyesight is poor, but their sense of smell is highly developed.

LOCATION/HABITAT

Lesser-spotted dogfish are the most common and widespread member of the dogfish (shark)

family and are found all around the UK and Ireland over clean sand, mud and mixed ground.

DIET/BAIT

Confirmed bottom feeders, eating small fish, molluscs, crabs and worms. They are frequently caught on mackerel strip.

British Records
Shore: 4lb 15oz 3dr.   **Boat: 4lb 9oz.**

FISH'N'TIPS

▶ *Lesser-spotted dogfish are most common between spring and autumn.*

Bull Huss or Greater-Spotted Dogfish
Scyliorhinus stellaris

IDENTIFICATION

Greater-spotted dogfish are better known as bull huss. Their back and sides vary from sandy brown to a dark grey-brown, but they always have a liberal coating of large dark spots. The skin texture is rough.

LOCATION/HABITAT

Resident all around the British Isles in deeper water than lesser-spotted dogfish and over rough or mixed ground, which can be close to shore.

DIET/BAIT

Flatfish, shellfish; they also hunt for crabs in harbours after dark. Any bait with a good scent (e.g. mackerel) works.

British Records
Shore: 19lb 14oz.
Boat: 22lb 4oz.

RIGHT *Bull huss are caught over rough ground from boats and rock marks that border deep water.*

Shark
Blue Shark
Prionace glauca

Blues are the most common of the four shark species that visit southern British and Irish coasts each summer. Blue sharks get their name from their coloration, though this fades to a dull grey after death. They hunt in packs, often close to the surface.

BELOW *Blues are the most common shark species found around the British Isles.*

British Record   Boat: 218lb.

Mako Shark
Isurus oxyrinchus

Makos are solitary sharks that are fast-moving and aggressive. They are identified by a long streamlined grey-blue body and a pointed snout. When hooked they often repeatedly leap clear of the water.

British Record   Boat: 500lb.

Porbeagle Shark
Lamna nasus

Porbeagle sharks have relatively short and thick grey-blue bodies with a distinctive V-shaped notch in the top part of the tail fin. Porbeagles travel in groups and will come very close to shore when hunting.

British Record   Boat: 507lb.

Thresher Shark
Alopias vulpinus

Threshers use their extremely long, scythe-like tails to herd and then disorientate shoals of fish, making them more vulnerable when attacked. Threshers hunt alone and have a habit of leaping from the water.

British Record   Boat: 323lb.

DIET/BAIT

All four shark species are voracious predators that feed on smaller species of fish, especially mackerel and herring.

BELOW *A specimen blue shark. The species' name derives from its coloration, though it quickly fades to grey after death.*

FISH'N'TIPS

▶ *Keep a constant stream of mashed-up mackerel going into the sea to attract sharks to the boat and hookbaits.*

Smooth Hounds

IDENTIFICATION

The smooth hound and starry smooth hound are close relatives and both are small members of the shark family. Both species are renowned for their fighting ability and, with their slim athletic builds and oversize fins, can show a remarkable turn of speed on being hooked.

Smooth hounds have light grey backs and flanks and yellow-white bellies. Starry smooth hounds show similar colouring, but in addition have a scattering of small white star-like spots on their backs.

LOCATION/HABITAT

Both smooth hound species inhabit inshore waters where the seabed consists of sand or gravel.

DIET/BAIT

Both species are bottom feeders with mouths equipped with flat teeth that are used to crush and grind crabs and shellfish. It can take some time before a smooth hound takes a bait properly into its mouth, making it advisable to resist striking at early indications of a bite and instead wait for the fish to move off. Ragworm and crab baits both work well.

Smooth hounds feed in packs and are most active at dusk and into dark, especially during hot and close weather.

British Records	
Smooth Hound	
(Mustelus mustelus)	
Shore: 20lb 3oz.	
Boat: 28lb.	
Starry Smooth Hound	
(Mustelus asterias)	
Shore: 23lb 2oz.	
Boat: 28lb 2oz.	

BELOW With their streamlined shape and large fins, starry smooth hounds are renowned for fighting hard and fast on being hooked.

RIGHT Smooth hounds can take time to ingest baits properly so allow them to move off before setting the hook.

Mackerel
Scomber scombrus

IDENTIFICATION

Related to tuna, mackerel are fantastic fighters for their size. Slim and solidly built, mackerel sport a vivid blue-green back overlaid with black barring, and an iridescent sheen over the pale flanks and belly.

LOCATION/HABITAT

A midwater to surface feeder that arrives off the coasts of the British Isles every summer in huge shoals. Mackerel will come into very shallow water to prey on small fish.

DIET/BAIT

Any small fish are eaten. Float-fished mackerel strip, feathers and small spinners work well.

British Records

Shore: 5lb 11oz 14dr.   Boat: 6lb 2oz 7dr.

LEFT Mackerel occur in vast shoals and are used as bait to catch numerous species.

Garfish
Belone belone

IDENTIFICATION

With its eel-like body and long, toothy beak, the garfish is instantly recognisable. Garfish resemble a fish from the tropics with their vibrant blue-green backs, silvery flanks and belly and habit of tail-walking when hooked.

LOCATION/HABITAT

Garfish arrive during early summer and are most common around the southern half of the UK and Ireland. They are often found with mackerel and will come close to shore, when they can be caught from rocky coastlines, piers and harbour walls.

DIET/BAIT

Garfish feed high in the water on small fish and will take float fished mackerel strip and sandeels.

British Records

Shore: 3lb 4oz 12dr.   Boat: 3lb 9oz 8dr.

FISH'N'TIPS

▶ *Garfish are excellent eating – despite the green bones!*

RIGHT Although garfish are aggressive top-water feeders, it can be difficult to secure a firm hook-hold in their long, narrow beaks.

Wrasse

Five species of wrasse occur around the British Isles, but only two are of interest to anglers: the ballan and cuckoo wrasse. The others – corkwing, goldsinny and rock-cook – weigh mere ounces.

Wrasse inhabit rugged coastlines; the Channel Islands, the West Country and the west of Ireland are top locations. Between spring and autumn they can be found close inshore, particularly where rocks and cliffs border deep water and heavy weed growth occurs.

Ballan Wrasse
Labrus bergylta

Deep-bodied and solid to the touch, ballan wrasse are ferocious fighters. Coloration varies with location and water clarity, but it is commonly dark olive across the back, lightening to a yellow-orange belly covered with white spots. The dorsal and anal fins are spiny. Ballan wrasse have powerful jaws and sharp teeth for ripping limpets and mussels from rocks, and also feed on crabs and prawns.

British Records.
Shore: 9lb 1oz.
Boat: 9lb 7oz 12dr.

Cuckoo Wrasse
Labrus mixus

Male and female cuckoo wrasse are markedly different in colour. Females are pale with a pinkish hue, males are bright yellow-orange with a blue head, blue stripes down both flanks and blue-edged fins.

DIET/BAIT
Cuckoo wrasse feed on worms, molluscs and crabs.

British Records
Shore: 1lb 12oz 9dr.
Boat: 2lb 7oz 12dr.

ABOVE *Male cuckoo wrasse are one of the most vividly coloured fish species to be found around the coasts of the British Isles.*

FISH'N'TIPS
▶ *Float fish deep gullies with small hardback crabs, prawns or worm baits – bites are often instant.*

LEFT *Corkwing wrasse live along rocky coastlines but never reach 1lb in weight.*

Flounder
Pleuronectes flesus

IDENTIFICATION
Coloration across the back ranges from light to dark brown, overlaid with darker blotches and small yellow-orange spots. Uniquely among flatfish, flounders have a row of small hard projections along the lateral line. Occasionally the white underside exhibits brown patches.

LOCATION/HABITAT
Flounders prefer sandy and muddy bottoms and are common all year round. In estuaries they will often swim well upstream into freshwater. River estuaries in south Devon provide excellent flounder fishing, while in Ireland they are also found off storm beaches.

DIET/BAIT
Flounders feed on worms, crabs and molluscs. Peeler crab is considered the best bait.

British Records
Shore: 5lb 7oz. **Boat: 5lb 11oz 8dr.**

LEFT Flounders are inquisitive. Add fluorescent beads to hooklengths to draw them to baits.

Plaice
Pleuronectes platessa

IDENTIFICATION
With their orange- or red-spotted brown backs, plaice are easy to identify.

FISH'N'TIPS
▶ *Add brightly coloured beads to hooklengths to attract plaice and flounder.*

LOCATION/HABITAT
Plaice are common throughout the British Isles and prefer relatively shallow water over fine shingle, sand or mud. While frequently caught from beaches, the larger specimens tend to be taken from offshore sandbanks. The Skerries (off Devon) and Shambles (off Dorset) sandbanks are renowned for producing big plaice.

DIET/BAIT
Particularly mussels, other shellfish, worms, small crustaceans. Mackerel strip, squid, lugworm and ragworm all work well.

British Records
Shore: 8lb 6oz 14dr. **Boat: 10lb 3oz 8dr.**

ABOVE Offshore sandbanks out from the south and south-west coasts regularly produce specimen plaice.

Dab
Limanda limanda

IDENTIFICATION
A small flatfish with both eyes on the right side of the head. the dab's upper body is yellow-brown in colour with brown spots. The underside is white. The dab's mouth is small and its skin feels rough if brushed from tail to head.

LOCATION/HABITAT
Common all around Britain and Ireland, over shallow sandy bottoms.

DIET/BAIT
Worms, shellfish and crab are all taken.

British Records
Shore: 2lb 9oz 8dr.   Boat: 2lb 12oz 4dr.

RIGHT *The dab, which rarely exceeds a foot in length, is the smallest representative of the flatfish clan. It makes an excellent table fish.*

Dover Sole
Solea solea

IDENTIFICATION
Dover sole are long and slim with a small head and mouth. The back is pale brown with darker patches and speckling. The underside is white. To aid identification there is a dark spot on the right pectoral fin.

LOCATION/HABITAT
Common on sandy and gravelly shores around the British Isles. They will feed very close to the water's edge after dark during settled spells of weather in summer.

DIET/BAIT
Small pieces of lugworm and ragworm.

British Records
Shore: 6lb 8oz 10dr.   Boat: 4lb 6oz.

Lemon Sole
Micro stomuskitt

The smaller lemon sole lives in similar habitats to the Dover sole, and on a similar diet, but it is much less frequently caught by anglers. It features similar colouring to the Dover sole but is smooth to the touch and more like a dab in shape.

British Records
Shore: 2lb 7oz 11dr.
Boat: 3lb 4oz 14dr.

RIGHT *Sole will move into very shallow water to feed. Bites should be left to develop as sole have small mouths, as shown on this Dover sole.*

FISH'N'TIPS
▶ *The beaches of East Anglia provide excellent fishing for dab and sole.*

Turbot
Scopthalmus maximus

RIGHT With their superb camouflage and large mouths, turbot can ambush and swallow small fish whole.

IDENTIFICATION
Turbot are a broad, thick-set voracious and hard-fighting flatfish with both eyes on the left side of the head. Body colour varies with the seabed, but is generally a sandy brown on top with scattered dark spots on body and tail and small bony tubercules.

LOCATION/HABITAT
Turbot are most common along south and south-western coasts and prefer a seabed of sand or shingle. While they can be found in quite shallow water in estuaries and particularly over offshore sandbanks, they also occur around deep water wrecks.

DIET/BAIT
Turbot prey on small flatfish, sand eels, sprats and shrimps. Fish on the drift with baits on long flowing traces.

British Records
Shore: 28lb 8oz.   Boat: 33lb 12oz.

FISH'N'TIPS
▶ *Turbot like to lie behind sandbanks and ambush small fish swept over them by the current.*

Brill
Scopthalmus rhombus

RIGHT Brill live in similar habitats to turbot but grow to only half their size.

IDENTIFICATION
Although the coloration is similar, the brill's body is narrower than that of its close relative the turbot, and does not have any tubercules on its back or spots on its tail. Like turbot, both eyes are on the left side of the head.

LOCATION/HABITAT
Very similar to turbot, though they can be found in faster and shallower water.

DIET/BAIT
Brill prey on small flatfish, sand eels, sprats and shrimps. Fish on the drift with baits on long flowing traces.

British Records
Shore: 7lb 7oz 8dr.   Boat: 16lb.

Thornback Ray
Raja clavata

IDENTIFICATION
Well named, due to the numerous short spikes over the upper body and tail. Colouring varies with habitat, from yellow-brown to grey-brown, with lighter scattered patches and black spotting.

LOCATION/HABITAT
Common throughout the British Isles. Thornbacks move into shallow water over sand, gravel or mud between spring and autumn.

DIET/BAIT
Fish baits and peeler crab. In East Anglia, hermit crab is popular.

British Records
Shore: 21lb 12oz. 　　　　　　　Boat: 31lb 7oz.

LEFT *Thornback rays travel in groups, and are scavengers that will eat a variety of food items, both living and dead, that they encounter.*

LEFT *The spines on the backs and tails of thornback rays can be very sharp and require careful handling.*

Common Skate
Raja batis

IDENTIFICATION
Common skate possess flat, diamond-shaped bodies, pointed snouts and long, thick tails covered in spines. Colour varies between green-brown and grey-brown. Common skate grow huge, with 100lb-plus specimens reported every year.

LOCATION/HABITAT
Off the west coasts of Scotland and Ireland and often in deep water over rough ground.

DIET/BAIT
Mainly fish – especially dogfish and pollack.

British Records
Shore: 169lb 6oz. 　　　　　　　Boat: 227lb.

RIGHT All skate caught today are returned after capture. Many are also tagged, in order that population numbers can be monitored.

FISH'N'TIPS
▶ *Mull in Scotland and Clew Bay in Ireland are the two hotspots for common skate.*

RIGHT Halibut are the biggest member of the flatfish family and are voracious feeders.

Halibut
Hippoglossus hippoglossus

IDENTIFICATION
Halibut are long, thick flatfish with an upper side coloured dark green-brown. The tail is big and powerful and the mouth filled with large teeth.

LOCATION/HABITAT
Halibut only occur around the north of Scotland, the Orkneys and Shetland, where they live in deep water with fast currents over rocky or broken ground.

DIET/BAIT
Fish – especially coalfish and squid.

British Record   Boat: 234lb.

Rays

FISH'N'TIPS

▶ *Most beach fishing for rays is done at night in calm conditions and from low water up.*

Rays are most common off south and south-western coasts during the summer. They prefer living over clean sandy or shingle seabeds and feed on small fish, crustaceans, shellfish and worms.

Spotted Ray
Raja montagui
Also known as a homelyn ray. A light brown back with large dark brown spots and a scattering of spines over the head and down the spine. Prefers deep water and not commonly caught.

British Records
Shore: 8lb 5oz.   Boat: 8lb 10oz 8dr.

Small-Eyed Ray
Raja microcellata
Also known as a painted ray, these are grey to yellow-brown on top, overlaid with large cream patches and streaks in line with the wing edges. Spines down the back.

British Records
Shore: 15lb 0oz 8dr.   Boat: 17lb 8oz.

Blonde Ray
Raja brackyura
An offshore species, preferring fast tide runs over sand and shingle banks. Yellow or light brown back, with paler patches covered in small brown spots and spines.

British Records
Shore: 32lb 8oz.   Boat: 39lb 10oz 2dr.

Cuckoo Ray
Raja naerus
A small species with a heart-shaped profile and distinctive black and yellow circular marks on either wing. The back and tail are grey-brown and covered with tiny spines.

British Records
Shore: 4lb 10oz.   Boat: 5lb 11oz.

Undulate Ray
Raja undulata
Back colour varies from brown to yellow-brown with irregular wavy dark markings edged in white or yellow.

British Records
Shore: 21lb 4oz.   Boat: 21lb 4oz 8dr.

Monkfish
Squatina squatina

With their flattened front end, wide pectorals resembling a skate, and shark-shaped lower body, monkfish appear to be a mixture of both species. Colouring is usually a mottled grey-brown, and the mouth is always huge and filled with sharp teeth.

Monkfish occur in small pockets around the south and south west of the British Isles and prefer shallow water over sandy or muddy seabeds where they feed on small fish, especially flatfish.

British Records
Shore: 52lb 14oz.   **Boat: 66lb.**

LEFT Despite growing large, monkfish usually put up little resistance when hooked.

Stingray
Dasyatis pastinaca

Stingrays are thick-set and smooth-bodied with a short snout and a rapidly tapering tail that possesses two long serrated spines coated in poison. Coloration is dark olive-grey or brown.

In summer, stingrays will move into very shallow water over a sandy or muddy bottom to feed on worms, shellfish and crabs. They are most common on south and east coasts.

British Records
Shore: 59lb 12oz 9dr.
Boat: 72lb 2oz.

FISH'N'TIPS

▶ *Turning a stingray on its back for unhooking keeps their stinging tail immobile.*

Eagle Ray
Myliobatis aquila

Eagle rays have wide, grey-brown triangular bodies, prominent heads and long whip-like tails. Their large mouths are filled with flattened teeth for crushing molluscs and crustaceans. They are occasionally caught off the south and south-west coasts by boat anglers fishing over sandy and muddy bottoms.

British Record
Boat: 101lb 14oz 14dr.

ABOVE Most eagle rays are caught more by accident than design off the south and south-west coasts of Britain and Ireland.

Silver Eel
Anguilla anguilla

IDENTIFICATION
Freshwater eels migrate to the sea in late summer and autumn to start the long journey to their spawning grounds in the mid-Atlantic. When living in lakes and rivers the eel is a yellow-brown colour but prior to migrating this evolves to a silvery bronze.

LOCATION/HABITAT
Silver eels are best targeted in estuaries as they make their way down to the sea. Eels are stimulated to run by heavy rainfall causing rivers to rise and colour up.

DIET/BAIT
Lugworm, ragworm, peeler crab, lobworm.

RIGHT Silver eels are caught during the late summer and autumn from many estuaries.

Conger Eel
Conger conger

FISH'N'TIPS
▶ *A mackerel head with the guts attached is a good bait for conger eels.*

IDENTIFICATION
Conger eels have dark, grey-brown backs and flanks lightening to silvery yellow bellies. The dorsal and anal fins are long and continuous and join at the tail. Congers have large eyes and very strong jaws.

LOCATION/HABITAT
Congers are found throughout the British Isles and offshore inhabit deep-water wrecks and reefs. Inshore, conger eels favour rocky coastlines and harbours where they can hide away in crevices and holes when not feeding. Shore-caught conger are usually smaller and feed better at night.

DIET/BAIT
Congers are voracious and feed on small fish, squid and crustaceans.

British Records

Shore: 68lb 8oz.	Boat: 133lb 4oz.

ABOVE Conger eels are incredibly tough and fight tenaciously – even after being landed!

Gurnard

Gurnards are odd-looking fish with large square heads and narrow bodies that taper rapidly to the tail. All three species have pectoral fins in which the first three rays are separate and are used as food-locating probes by the fish as they move across the seabed.

Tub Gurnard
Trigla lucerna

Tub gurnard are vividly coloured with a pink or red back and flanks, yellow underside and blue pectoral fins edged in red and spotted in white or green. They are found throughout UK waters over a sandy or muddy seabed, and feed in groups on bottom-dwelling fish, crabs and shellfish.

British Records
Shore: 12lb 3oz.
Boat: 11lb 7oz 4dr.

Grey Gurnard
Eutrigla gurnardus

Grey gurnard have grey-brown backs and a pink tinge to their flanks, which are sometimes covered with white spots. The short front dorsal fin sports a large black spot. They are widely distributed and inhabit bottoms offering a mixture of rocks, mud and sand. Grey gurnard feed on small fish and crustaceans.

British Records
Shore: 1lb 10oz 8dr.
Boat: 2lb 7oz.

Red Gurnard
Aspitrigla cuculus

Red gurnard are bright red along the back with paler flanks. They live over similar ground to and share a similar diet with grey gurnard.

British Record
Shore: 2lb 10oz 11dr.
Boat: 2lb 14oz 10dr.

ABOVE *Red gurnard have the coloration of a tropical species. Beware their sharp spines when handling them.*

ABOVE *A grey gurnard – with eyes bigger than its stomach – that took a pirk.*

Black Bream
Spondyliosoma cantharus

IDENTIFICATION
Deep bodied, the black bream sports a black back with a blue sheen and silvery grey flanks overlaid with a row of dark vertical stripes. The long dorsal fin is tipped with sharp spines, and the tail is deeply forked. The head and mouth are small and the upper jaw equipped with two rows of numerous sharp teeth. Although not growing to any great size, black bream are renowned for their fighting ability.

LOCATION/HABITAT
Black bream are a shoal fish that inhabit rough ground, reefs and wrecks off the south coast of England and are caught virtually exclusively by boat anglers fishing during the summer.

DIET/BAIT
Crab and small fish, sand eels, squid.

British Records
Shore: 6lb 8oz 6dr.   **Boat: 6lb 14oz 4dr.**

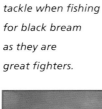

BELOW *Use light tackle when fishing for black bream as they are great fighters.*

Red Bream
Pagellus bogaraveo

FISH'N'TIPS

▶ *A squid/ragworm cocktail will catch both black and red bream.*

IDENTIFICATION
Mature red bream are orangey red in colour, with silvery pink flanks and grey fins. There is also a black patch just behind each gill cover. The dorsal fin is long and spiny, and their large eyes show them to be a fish of deep water.

LOCATION/HABITAT
Deep water, rough ground – especially off the south-west coast of England. Red bream rise towards the surface to feed as daylight fades.

DIET/BAIT
Molluscs, crab and small fish.

British Records
Shore: 4lb 7oz.   **Boat: 9lb 8oz 12dr.**

Gilthead Bream
Sparus aurata

IDENTIFICATION
Silvery flanks with a typical deep-bodied bream shape. Giltheads develop a characteristic gold patch across the eyes as they mature. The mouth is filled with lines of small grinding teeth.

LOCATION/HABITAT
A summer visitor to southern shores and now common along the south coast of Ireland, where they move into shallow sandy bays to feed.

DIET/BAIT
Mussels, razorfish, crab, lugworm, oysters.

British Records
Shore: 10lb 5oz 8dr.
Boat: 9lb 15oz 8dr.

RIGHT Like all members of the bream family, giltheads are great fighters and also make excellent eating.

Couch's Sea Bream
Sparus pagnus

IDENTIFICATION
Deep silver-pink body with pale pink fins. The mouth is equipped with front cutting teeth and rear crushers.

LOCATION/HABITAT
Shoals appear during the summer off southern coasts of the British Isles.

DIET/BAIT
Mussels, limpets, clams.

British Records
Shore: 2lb 15oz 1dr.
Boat: 6lb 9oz 7dr.

ABOVE Couch's sea bream are extending their range northwards and are expected to become more common as sea temperatures rise.

Triggerfish
Balistes capriscus

IDENTIFICATION
Dark grey, thick-set flat body; the small mouth behind thick lips is filled with sharp teeth, and a small spiky front dorsal fin.

LOCATION/HABITAT
Increasingly common along rocky south and south-western shores of Britain and Ireland during the summer.

DIET/BAIT
Triggerfish use their sharp teeth to remove limpets from rocks and crush any other shellfish and crustaceans encountered. Limpets, mussels and crab are taken.

British Records
Shore: 5lb 14oz 8dr.
Boat: 6lb 4oz 14dr.

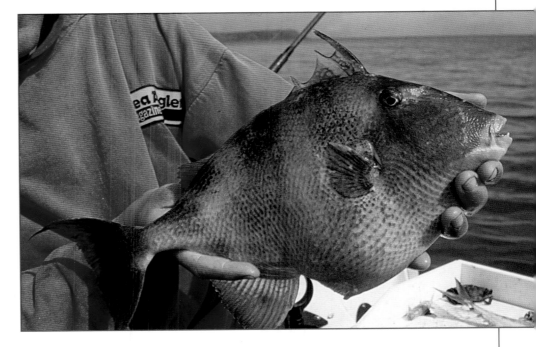

ABOVE Although triggerfish have small mouths, they can prise limpets from rocks with their powerful jaws and sharp teeth.

Artificial Sea Baits
Spoons, Spinners and Plugs

Spoons are most commonly used in sea fishing on rigs designed to catch flatfish. Flounders, plaice, turbot and brill are all attracted to the fluttering action of a spoon, particularly where it kicks up sand or clouds of silt from the seabed. It is thought the action of the spoon imitates a small flatfish near the hookbait or a crab scuttling along the bottom, as both would be attractive food to a larger flatfish.

When fished on a rig from a boat, a spoon will readily revolve in the tidal flow, but from a beach, action will have to be imparted to it and the rig should therefore be slowly reeled in across the bottom to create a disturbance.

Spoons for flatfish rigs are available in plastic and metal, from one inch up to around four inches long and in many different colours, including really bright fluorescent shades.

From rock marks, spoon lures are most often used to target pollack and mackerel; slim bar spoons measuring four to five inches long, to imitate sand eels, work best. Attaching a large spoon to the end of a trace of feathers, instead of to a lead for casting weight, often sees a bonus bigger fish hooked.

Small spinners with revolving blades, such as the famous Mepps series, are successful for thin-lipped mullet. The treble hook at the rear of the spinner should be tipped with a short section of ragworm, as this appears to be as attractive to the mullet as the spinning blade.

Although plugs will catch a number of different saltwater species, they are most commonly associated

FISH'N'TIPS

▶ *Keep mobile while lure fishing and carry a Gye net, originally designed for salmon fishing, on your back for landing any big fish hooked.*

with bass. The best times to fish for bass with plugs is at dawn and dusk, when light values are low and bass are more confident. Surface poppers, floating divers and sinking plugs will all take bass on the right day. Jointed plugs possess a more exaggerated action. Use silver-blue and silver-green colour combinations that imitate mackerel, sea trout and sand eels.

Bass can be caught on plugs from rocky marks (particularly those with heavy weed growth harbouring numerous food items), estuaries and even open beaches, where it pays to wade to reach deeper water.

Ensure plugs are fitted with corrosion-resistant treble hooks – but still rinse them thoroughly in fresh water after use.

Pirks and Muppets

Pirks are heavy lures weighing up to 1lb (sometimes more) that rapidly sink to the seabed under their own weight, used from boats to catch species like ling, pollack, coalfish and cod over rough ground or shipwrecks.

Most commercially produced pirks are tubular, though some are made with a simple fish outline and even have scale patterning built into their sides.

Pirks are effective for catching fish, but they are not cheap, and losses over snaggy wrecks can be high, either through the lure catching up on part of the superstructure, or a big fish diving on it and breaking the line.

Consequently, many sea anglers make their own pirks from lengths of chrome tubing (old prams are ideal). After being cut to size, up to a foot long, the tubing is filled with molten lead. When the lead has set, a hole is drilled through each end and a large split ring is threaded through. A swivel is attached to one end and a big treble hook to the other.

Tackle losses can be reduced by tying the treble hook at the base of the pirk to a short length of line that is a slightly lighter breaking strain. Then, if it becomes snagged only the treble will be lost rather than the whole pirk.

Pirks are lowered close to the wreck or reef then jerked up and down by repeatedly raising and lowering the rod tip, keeping the line tight at all times. Bites can be savage and fights hard; a day spent working a pirk and hauling big fish up from the depths is not for the unhealthy!

Muppets are rubber lures that resemble an octopus or squid. They are available in many different sizes and colours, including ones with light-reflecting glitter through the head and tentacles.

Large muppets are often fished on the treble hook of a pirk for added attraction. To mount one, the treble has to be removed from the pirk and pushed up through a hole made in the head of the muppet. The treble is then

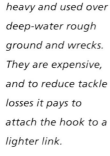

BELOW Pirks are heavy and used over deep-water rough ground and wrecks. They are expensive, and to reduce tackle losses it pays to attach the hook to a lighter link.

RIGHT Large muppets (often attached to pirks) and eels are normally fished singly, while smaller versions are rigged up in teams of three or more.

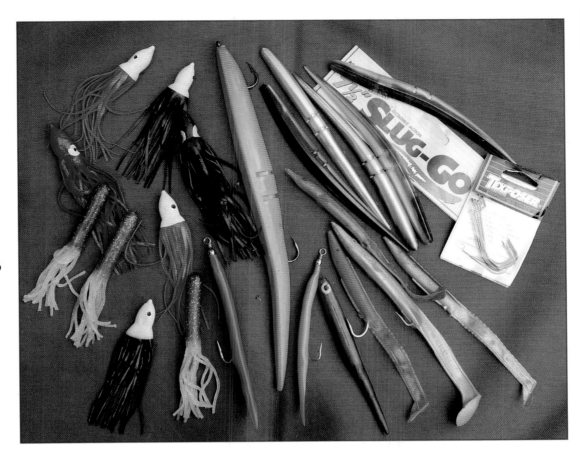

reattached to the pirk with its three hook points protruding through the muppet's tentacles.

Smaller muppets are usually sold in packs – either loose or attached to a trace. These teams, usually of three or more, are weighted by a lead or pirk at the base of the trace and, like pirks, are fished over wrecks and rough ground.

Feathers, Eels and Worms

While feathers are primarily associated with mackerel, they will take other species, too. They are produced in a wide variety of colours, and today many are made from shiny plastic and foil as well as natural feathers.

Feathers are sold on traces and are designed to imitate a shoal of small fish. A team of six is more than enough to handle when fishing from a shore mark or out in a boat. Many commercially produced feathers

FISH'N'TIPS
▶ Make muppets more attractive by attaching fish strips to the hooks.

▶ Ensure pirks remain shiny by regularly polishing them.

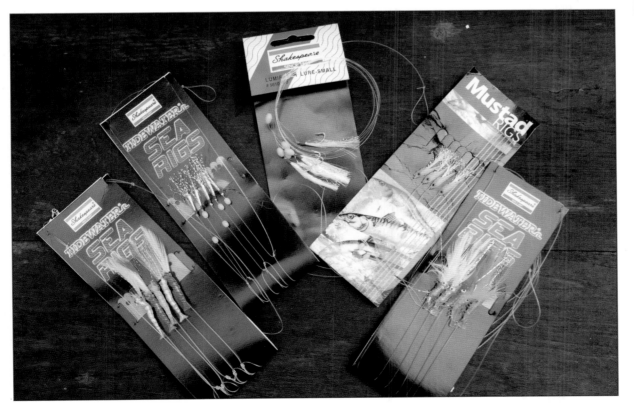

LEFT Feathers are most often associated with mackerel, but they can be used to catch many other species as well.

FISH'N'TIPS

intended for mackerel are too large and result in missed takes. Look for those tied on smaller hooks (2–1/0) with their feathers just extending beyond the hook.

When feathering for mackerel it pays to crush the hooks' barbs. This makes unhooking the mackerel much easier, and should a bare hook on the trace catch you, it is a simple matter to pull it out. While some mackerel will inevitably shed the hook or drop off in the water, normally there are plenty more willing to grab the feathers.

BELOW *Rubber and plastic eels, shads and worms are produced in a huge range of shapes, sizes and colours and can be used to great effect from boat or shore.*

Whereas coloured and silvery feathers will account for mackerel and pollack, cod prefer white feathers. Herring are also caught occasionally on white feathers.

Rubber eels are great fish catchers and most commonly used from boats for pollack, ling, coalfish and bass. They are intended to imitate either the common sand eel or the much larger greater sand eel or launce, and are produced in sizes ranging from a couple of inches up to more than a foot long.

Their solid bodies taper to a very slim tail section that ends in a thick stump. This stump causes the eel's tail to wag vigorously in the current, sending out fish-attracting vibrations.

From a boat, eels are usually fished singly on a long trace, which allows them to work attractively in the flow. When used from the shore for bass and pollack they are cast and retrieved.

Plastic worms are available in a variety of sizes and colours and are effective for many species either from the shore or afloat. While their bodies are round, the tails are flattened and on some models are curled to further increase the movement. Retrieve them with a sink and draw action.

Plastic worms are hooked through the head. Special weighted hooks, with lead moulded around the eye and top of the shank, can be used to take them down, or a weight can be attached further up the trace with the worm attached to a conventional hook.

Natural Sea Baits
Fish and Squid

Mackerel are a widely used bait for everything from flatfish to sharks. They can be caught on spinners and feathers from rock marks, piers and breakwaters during the summer, bought fresh from supermarkets or blast (quick) frozen from tackle shops.

When fished from the beach or rocks, bait mackerel is most commonly used in strips. A fillet is taken from one side of a mackerel – use a sharp knife and slice from behind the gill cover to the indentation above the tail – then cut into strips. Float-fish strips for garfish and mackerel and leger them for species like dogfish and whiting on hook sizes 2–1/0.

Whole fillets make excellent baits for cod and bass. Flappers are mackerel from which the backbone has been removed leaving the head and flanks, which flap in a current. They are hooked through the head (6/0–8/0) and used from boats to catch conger, tope and sharks. Live mackerel are also used for catching sharks, while a mackerel head legered in the surf can account for big bass during the winter months.

Two species of sand eel are to be found around the British Isles. The more common lesser sand eel grows to around 7 inches, whereas the greater sand eel, or launce, can exceed one foot. If sand eels can be obtained alive, they are a great bait to float fish for wrasse and garfish. Keep them in a bucket of seawater fitted with an aerator.

FISH'N'TIPS

▶ Try a combination of baits on the hook – "cocktails" are more appealing to many species.

BELOW A mackerel's head and flanks – known as a flapper, as it flaps in the current – is used to catch tope, conger eels and sharks.

LEFT Three greater sand eels taken on feathers. Normally, the first task of the day when out on a boat trip is to use feathers to catch fresh bait.

FISH'N'TIPS

▸ *Keep fish baits in a cool box or bag with freezer blocks to ensure they remain fresh throughout a session.*

▸ *Rig up sand eels on hooklengths at home then freeze them ready for use.*

RIGHT Blast (fast) frozen fish, crabs and molluscs are widely available from tackle shops and are a highly convenient, if rather expensive, way to secure a selection of baits.

Blast-frozen sand eels are widely available from tackle shops. For a top presentation thread the line through a sand eel from head to tail with a baiting needle then attach a long shank Aberdeen hook. Tighten the line to pull the hook inside the sand eel, leaving just the bend and point exposed.

For distance casting bind the sand eel with bait elastic. For smaller sand eels use a size 1 or 1/0 hook, but for big sand eels (launce) a hook as large as a 5/0 may be necessary. Change sand eels after every cast and add extra flavour by combining them with mackerel strip. Sand eels will catch numerous species from the shore including a variety of flatfish, pollack, dogfish and bass.

Squid can be bought frozen from tackle shops and are either small "calamaris" or a much larger species up to 2ft long. Calamari squid are around 6 inches long and can be used whole for bass, rays, conger eel and cod when fishing in deep water from a boat. Fish them on a two-hook (3/0–6/0) pennell rig for a natural presentation.

For smaller species, when fishing ashore or afloat, use either species of squid, cut into strips to wave enticingly in the tidal flow. Skinning the squid will reveal the clean white flesh that many fish can't resist. It is an excellent bait for whiting, black bream and codling. Squid is often combined with another bait to make a cocktail.

Lugworms and Ragworms

Lugworms and ragworms can either be bought from coastal tackle shops or dug from the shore for free. The best time to dig is at low water and especially on spring tides when the sea recedes further exposing even more beds. Store worms on a shallow seawater-filled tray in the fridge. Any dead or dying worms should be removed and the water changed daily.

The night before fishing, wrap the worms in newspaper. Drying the worms toughens them up making them less likely to fly off the hook during casting.

Black lugworms are found on muddy beaches and estuaries and can lie several feet below the surface, making digging hard work.

The more common blow lugworms are a reddish-brown colour and are found on beaches of sand, mud or shale, or a mixture of materials.

Look for an area where a good number of casts exist, then dig a trench rather than try and target individual worms. Build up the sides with dug material to keep water out. Blow lugworms lie nearer the surface in summer, and are rarely ever more than a foot below the surface.

If using lugworms straight after digging, retain them in a bucket and cover them with seawater. Fresh lugworms are soft, so thread on several when fishing at distance to ensure the hook is still carrying the bait when it reaches the seabed.

LEFT Typical lugworm casts. Dig where a good concentration occurs. The best time is at low water and especially on big spring tides when additional beds will be exposed.

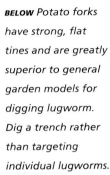

BELOW Potato forks have strong, flat tines and are greatly superior to general garden models for digging lugworm. Dig a trench rather than targeting individual lugworms.

ABOVE Ragworms can grow up to 24 inches long and lie as much as 2ft below the surface of shingle and mud beaches, which can make collecting them hard work.

BELOW A fisherman is seen collecting peeler crabs at low tide. The bucket, which has had holes cut in the bottom, allows the water to drain. In this way any crabs, or other bait, remain in the bucket.

FISH'N'TIPS

▶ King ragworms have sharp pincers that can give a painful nip – beware!

▶ Lugworms will catch fish even from beaches where they do not occur.

RIGHT Fish a worm bait close behind a freely revolving spoon to attract flatfish. Being inquisitive, they are quickly attracted to the fluttering motion, then spot the worm.

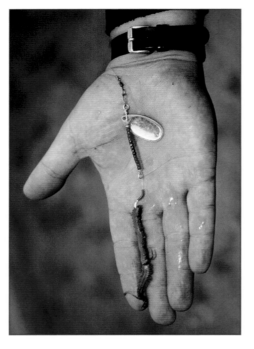

Lugworms are an excellent bait for many species including flatfish, cod, whiting and dogfish. Hook size is dependent on the species sought.

King ragworms live in mixed beaches of shingle, shale and mud and can grow up to 2ft long! Look for holes that squirt water as you walk close by and be prepared to dig as much as 2ft to find the worms. Thread king ragworms onto 1/0–4/0 long shank hooks and leave the tail hanging free for its movement to entice fish. King ragworms will catch many species including flatfish and bass.

Harbour ragworms (also known as maddies and reds) are small and best fished in bunches on long shank hook sizes 1–4. They are excellent for mullet, bass and flounders. White ragworms are also small and are highly prized by match anglers. They are often found with lugworms and appeal to many species. Fish them the same way as harbour ragworms.

FISH'N'TIPS

▶ *Store ragworms in newspaper in the fridge. If they are not being used immediately, check them regularly and discard any that are dead or dying.*

Shellfish and Prawns

Razorfish are an excellent bait and will catch dabs, plaice, flounders, brill, whiting, codling and bass. They can be bought frozen or collected from sandy shorelines. Dead low water on big spring tides is the best time; go armed with a supply of salt. Tread quietly and pour salt down holes left by burrowing razorfish, and they will soon pop up to the surface. Grip them tightly until they relax their hold then pull them from the sand. Pulling too hard will break off the fleshy foot – the most

prized part of the bait. Lever the two shells apart with a blunt knife and cut out the flesh. Thread razorfish onto an appropriate sized hook with the foot on last to help keep the bait in place. Razorfish can be dug out, but they burrow rapidly, making it hard work.

Clams are a great bait for bass in particular and can be dug at the low water mark on sandy beaches. Use them in the same way as mussels and cockles.

Pick the largest mussels you can find – either in the wild or in a supermarket – as they will contain the most flesh. Force the two shells apart with a blunt knife and then cut the mussel free. Mussels are extremely soft, and need to be lashed to the hook shank with bait elastic. Mussels will catch cod, coalfish, whiting, pouting and bass. Fish them on appropriately sized hooks.

Cockles lie just below the surface on shingle beaches and in estuaries, and are easily collected at the bottom of the tide with a garden rake. Thread several onto small hooks (sizes 6–1) for dabs, pouting, whiting and plaice. Cockles are good as part of a cocktail bait.

With their dome-shaped shells, limpets can be found in large colonies clinging to rocks. They are best removed with a sharp blow from a hard object. The flesh is tough and stays on the hook well. They are taken

RIGHT Baiting a drop net with mackerel is an excellent way to catch prawns, shrimps, crabs (including hermits) and small fish for use as bait.

avidly by wrasse. Bait a size 1/0 or 2/0 hook with around half a dozen limpets.

Slipper limpets are a larger shellfish that live on shingle beaches. Their flesh is softer and is a good bait for flatfish like dabs and flounders. Fish them on small hooks.

Prawns can be caught from rock pools with a small net or in a drop net baited with mackerel and lowered down a harbour wall. Retain prawns in a bucket with an aerator and float fish them for wrasse, pollack and mackerel in summer.

Crabs

Crabs feature heavily in the diet of many fish species and are one of the most popular baits used by sea anglers.

To be able to grow, crabs need to shed their shells periodically. During the period between the old and new hard shells, crabs are soft-bodied and vulnerable, and hide away under rocks and in crevices.

Soft-bodied crabs are easy to identify, while on those about to peel, the shell will be seen to be coming away near the legs. Lift it gently and it will come off, revealing the crab's soft back. The hardening process takes about a week, depending on air and water temperature, and can be slowed in collected peelers by storing them in a fridge. Keep them in a bucket and cover with damp seaweed. Change the weed every few days and remove any dead crabs.

When baiting with peeler crab, first peel off the old hard top shell, then remove the gills (under the eyes) and finally the legs and claws (retain and use as bait when the bodies run out). Small crabs can be used whole but larger specimens should be cut in half. Peeler crab is soft and needs to be bound on the hook shank with bait elastic. Threading the hook through the leg sockets can give added security. Hook size will depend on the species being targeted, but use wide gape patterns to prevent the point being masked.

If you live by a quiet beach or backwater inhabited by crabs, collecting peelers and soft backs can be made easier by placing old car tyres down at the low water mark. Alternatively, push wide-necked plastic tubs or plastic piping into muddy banks. Crabs will soon begin to use them for peeling.

Hardback crabs, measuring about one inch across the shell, are an excellent bait for wrasse. Hook them through a back leg and fish them a foot or so from the bottom, either under a sliding float or legered on a paternoster rig.

Shore crabs can be collected from under weed-covered rocks at low tide or in a drop net baited with mackerel lowered over the side of a pier or harbour wall. Hermit crabs live under stones and rocks and make their home in discarded whelk shells. Pull them out carefully and fish them whole on a large single hook. Sometimes tipped with ragworm, they are an excellent bait for cod, bass, thornbacks and flatfish.

LEFT Peeler crab is a highly prized bait that will catch many species. Being soft, it needs to be lashed to the hook shank with elastic thread.

LEFT Small hardback crabs are a first-rate bait for wrasse. Hook them through a back leg and fish them on or close to the bottom.

FISH'N'TIPS

▶ Both species of limpet also work well as part of a cocktail bait.

▶ The toughest part of all shellfish is the "foot". Push the hook through it for a firmer hook hold.

Shore Fishing
Rocks

MAIN PICTURE Rock marks often give access to deep water and to species usually caught only by anglers afloat. Explore at low water for bait, features and snags.

Fishing from rocks can produce a wide variety of species and the deeper water found at these marks means that very often the state of tide is less important. Bigger fish and deep-water species are accessible as well as exotic migrants like triggerfish in summer. Classic rough-ground species include pollack, ballan wrasse, conger eels and even bass. In winter the same marks may offer other species like full-sized cod, albeit in fiercely different conditions, when swapping sun cream for flotation suits will be necessary!

Survey rock marks at low water and note features for future reference – deep gullies,

holes, rocks that generate currents and potential snags. Exposed pools offer fresh bait in the form of crabs, shrimps, small fish, mussels and limpets and also illustrate the local fishes' diet. Lower a drop net baited with mackerel into weedy gullies or use a push net to collect bait from rock pools. Check the drop net regularly to ensure a conger eel is not eating the mackerel or the potential baits also attracted to it. During the summer, feathering for mackerel is normally productive and will provide plenty of bait for various species. To be on the safe side,

though, pack a chopping board, filleting knife and back-up frozen bait, just in case fresh bait is in short supply or unavailable.

Fishing with a selection of lures is a good way to explore new marks quickly. Use a 10ft spinning rod, preferably telescopic, or a multi-section travel model, as they will be easier to carry over rough terrain. Braid can be used with care but monofilament's resistance to abrasion from rocks and barnacles makes it a better choice. A fluorocarbon hooklength added to the end of the main line will increase takes when lure fishing, and

FISH'N'TIPS

▶ *Spinning can be highly effective along a rocky shore, with plugs and spoons accounting for a variety of species.*

INSET Replace treble hooks for singles or doubles on lures to reduce snagging in weed.

a snap swivel allows for rapid lure changes. Replace treble hooks on lures with singles or doubles to reduce snagging and, if you wish, use lure savers. Lure savers are engineered split rings, designed for different breaking strains. If the line gets snagged they release, so that only the hook is lost and not the expensive lure.

Look for white water boils and current streaks. Pollack ambush fish swept into eddies, and will come right inshore into darkness on flooding tides. German Sprats, Tobies, Dexter Wedges and even Flying Cs work, though persistent use of metal lures does scare off fish. On very deep-water marks or off cliffs, pirks and jigs can be effective. The shad's design, with the hook emerging at the top from its back, lets it bounce off most snags; adding a pike spinner makes them even more attractive to pollack. Soft plastic lures can also often produce takes, with fire tail jellies. A sand eel fished six feet behind a small lead, spun slowly just above kelp in a sink and draw action, is ideal for pollack.

Bass like similar territory to pollack, but will nose around quiet gullies, too, and over weedy rough ground. Here, floating and surface popper lures excel. Bass are easily spooked – avoid casting a shadow and keep out of sight.

Float fishing minimises tackle losses but it is important to adjust the depth at which the bait is fishing to allow for the tide. Check your survey to establish where those important gullies, rocks and holes are located. Ragworm and mackerel strip are classic float fishing baits. Trim ragworm to leave a small "tail" wriggling. Crab and limpets will attract wrasse and triggerfish. With hardback crabs, remove a rear leg and insert the hook, bringing it out through the carapace. Then, push a small piece of thick elastic band past the barb to stop fish sucking the bait off. Hook soft limpets through the "foot" then bind them with bait elastic. Float-fishing sand eels works in rough water, presenting the bait as though it has been stunned through impact with the rocks. Snip off the tail and the head above the eyes. Strips of squid attract coalfish and bream. Dogfish, flatfish and gurnard will all take float-fished baits so long as they are presented near the seabed. Mackerel strip and sand eels trotted downtide will account for more mackerel and garfish.

BELOW During the summer, numerous species can be caught from rock marks including pollack, wrasse, garfish, mackerel, conger eels and bass.

ABOVE Pollack are one of the most common species occurring along rocky coastlines and will engulf any lure or float fished bait.

To leger baits, use 30lb line and leads you do not mind losing – spark plugs or small rocks superglued to old weak monofilament will do. Use weak bottom links like paperclips to release quickly if snagging occurs. Long beachcaster rods will help you to land the fish safely by allowing you to keep further back from big waves. Distance casting lets you fish past the rough ground out into deeper waters where there may well be sandy patches. Fishing clipped-down or pulley rigs at distance brings bigger fish and different species into range. A popular aerodynamic bait is a whole squid body stuffed with lugworm – it casts well and is fairly crab resistant. In winter this bait can produce full-grown cod off the North Sea and painted rays around the Cornish coast.

Only a boat rod can properly handle conger eels, bull huss and other large species hooked from rock marks. For conger eels, start with two swivels above a 6/0 hook holding a mackerel head. Wire or 100lb line is used for the biting trace. Using a big pirk to aid handling the fish is popular in Ireland.

Balloon rigs let prevailing currents or winds sweep big baits far offshore – this method has worked for sharks and recently accounted for a skate exceeding 200lb in Scotland!

Rock marks and the sea demand respect. Travelling over rough terrain to reach marks can be physically demanding so wear hill-walking boots for a sure grip, rather than Wellingtons. Socks featuring padded toes and heels prevent blisters. Mountaineering rucksacks are ideal for a rocky terrain, or in good summer weather, travel really light with just a waist pack. Be prepared for bad

BELOW Always keep well back from the water's edge and use a long-handled net or drop net to land bigger fish.

weather; take breathable waterproofs and don't forget a hat in cold conditions. Bring plenty of water in sports cap bottles and/or hot drinks in flasks. Chocolate and other higher energy foods are essential.

Some anglers go to extraordinary lengths for their fishing. On Torr Head in Northern Ireland, someone has built their own concrete platform with galvanised rails and seats – the only problem facing anyone wishing to fish there is the long and difficult climb down… and back up again!

FISH'N'TIPS

▶ *Big floats are more visible in choppy seas or at a distance on sunny days.*

Storm Beaches

Western coasts are subjected to the full ferocity of Atlantic storms, and their beaches are often shallow and appear devoid of marine life.

Storm beaches are best fished in darkness, when fish will move into the clear, shallow water. Appalling weather is surprisingly helpful, for fearsome white-capped breakers will smash up small fish, crabs and marine life, presenting predators with free food. Fish after the storm has passed and conditions are improving. Bass and flatfish hunt in very shallow water and can be caught in ankle-deep water. Gullies, banks, groynes, odd rocks and scours create hot spots; note features at low water but remember they may not be there after the next storm. Streams are another key feature to look out for, attracting bass and flatfish in summer, but avoid them when in winter flood as the cold and often coloured water puts all fish off feeding.

Wading on these shallow beaches is essential to cast the baits out to or beyond the third breaker: a key position. In winter a flotation suit or jacket over chest waders and a life jacket are essential. Bass, especially, will feed in the "foam". Flatfish will be there, too: expect flounders, plaice, dabs, possibly turbot and brill. In winter, codling will hunt whiting feeding at or past the third breaker, and will have big bass for competition. Dogfish and rays are possible, as are bull huss, pollack, coalfish, wrasse and conger eels if there is foul ground offshore. Mixed shoals of mackerel and launce will often drive sprat up onto the sand in summer, and in turn will attract bass to the harvest. Look for terns diving close to shore.

Effective baits include lugworm, peeler crab, mackerel strip, sand eels, squid strip and ragworm – even when they do not occur on the beach being fished. Cocktail baits also work well: try ragworm or lugworm with sand eel, peeler crab and mackerel strip.

Use a two-hook flapper rig for short- to medium-range work and add coloured beads to the hooklengths when targeting flatfish. At or beyond the third breaker a host of species are available to bigger baits presented on pulley rigs, including small-eyed rays in Cornwall in the winter. Other rays prefer the summer, with spotted (homelyn) rays and thornbacks common at that time. To spin or fly-fish these beaches for bass, first let the sediment clear after a storm. Dawn and dusk are the most productive times to fish.

BELOW Bass fishing on an Irish storm beach. Bass will move into water only inches deep in search of food.

LEFT *Landing a good cod from the surf. Cod prefer to remain in deeper water when feeding, making long-distance casting necessary to reach them.*

Estuaries

River estuaries are often sheltered environments and rich feeding grounds for many species of fish, making them excellent fishing locations from both the shore and afloat.

Fish move into estuaries to feed as the tide rises, and the best time to fish them is the two hours up to high tide and the first two hours of the ebb. However, arrive earlier and dig for and collect bait for the coming session.

LEFT Although most estuary tope are caught from boats, they will regularly come within casting range of the shore.

ABOVE While pieces of freshwater eel oozing blood are an excellent bait for tope, they are regularly picked up by estuary bass, too.

BELOW During the summer bass move into estuaries to prey on shoals of small fish and sand eels.

With their tolerance of freshwater, flounders and mullet are the most common species found in estuaries. Prebaiting with mashed bread in summer can lead to the capture of thick-lipped mullet on breadflake, while a small ragworm-tipped spinner will account for thin lips. Flounders love peeler crab but will also take worm baits. They can be

caught all year round but are in best condition during the winter.

In summer, bass will move into estuaries to chase shoals of brit and sand eels and the presence of the bait fish is usually revealed by diving terns. Try legering sand eels, or try small lures.

Estuaries are normally snag free, making a light beach outfit practical. Use a 12ft beachcaster or bass rod designed to cast 2 to 4oz leads and a reel loaded with 15lb line. Hook-lengths need only be 10lb to 12lb breaking strain.

In the Thames and other large, deep estuaries, charter boat and dinghy anglers target tope with sections of freshwater eel and smooth hounds with ragworm or peeler and hermit crab. Bass will also be present and can be caught intentionally on sand eels, though they do also take eel baits intended for tope. Local prey fish, like whiting and poor cod, can

be used to catch blonde rays and thornbacks (roker), but use large hooks and baits to prevent the hordes of dogfish usually present from taking them.

New species like gilthead bream are becoming common along the south coast of Britain and Ireland, especially in estuaries with extensive eel grass beds. Stingrays hunt in shallow, sun-warmed, muddy and sandy waters and can be taken on ragworm, while several massive electric rays have also been landed from estuaries in recent times.

Piers, Breakwaters and Harbours

Piers are great venues for children and novices, offering easy fishing for a variety of species. In summer, mackerel will be the main target during the day and can be caught on spinners and feathers fished on a freshwater spinning rod, or on a fish bait presented under a float using an Avon rod.

At night big bass often move close to piers to feed on the small fish that congregate around and under the structure. Catch small pouting and pollack on float-fished mackerel strip and then float-fish them in turn as bait for the bass. Some floats accept a starlight for night fishing, though many piers are illuminated after dark. Alternatively, try for the bass with legered peeler crab or the head of a mackerel.

Legering a short distance out from the pier with lugworm or ragworm will account for many different species through the year including pollack, coalfish, whiting, codling and, if the pier is sited over sand, flounders, dabs and plaice.

LEFT Piers and breakwaters provide anglers with access to deeper water and a variety of species.

FISH'N'TIPS

▶ *Rats carry Weil's disease and love harbours, so wash your hands thoroughly with a medical cleanser such as Hibiscrub after fishing.*

▶ *When fishing from harbour walls, always watch out for rogue waves and the wake from big vessels.*

A standard beachcasting outfit with a two- or three-hook flapper rig will be perfectly fine.

Harbours attract mullet from spring through to autumn, and baiting with mashed bread will soon see them confidently taking breadflake hookbaits. Mullet frequenting harbours in which commercial fishing boats and charter boats moor up will often take fish baits, having become used to a regular free supply. Float fish baits on a stepped-up freshwater match rod and a reel loaded with 5 to 6lb line.

In the height of summer, harbour breakwaters can be busy with anglers catching mackerel, but other species are there to be caught as well. The seabed out from breakwaters is often rough, and this, combined with strong currents, will attract wrasse,

pollack, garfish, coalfish, dogfish, whiting, and codling – and sometimes even black bream. Dropping fish baits straight down into the holes in the wall can account for anything from a "piece of rubbish" to a specimen conger. When spinning or float-fishing, a short cast will reach the white-water boils and current streaks which attract predators.

Legering is possible but breakwaters are tackle graveyards. If you do leger, use a single hook and leads you do not mind losing. Distance-casting off breakwaters may get past the rocks and on to less-rugged ground (even sand) and deeper water. Then, anything is possible: skate, smooth hounds, stingrays and tope are landed from some marks around the coast.

Open Beaches

Open beaches are mostly composed of sand or shingle, or a mixture of both. They are often interspersed at regular intervals by wooden or concrete groynes jutting out to sea to slow the drift of beach materials along the coast. They also slope more steeply than storm beaches, resulting in less distance between the high and low water marks and making long-range casting less necessary to reach a reasonable depth of water.

These more benign environments allow life beneath the waves to flourish, and extensive beds of worm and large populations of shellfish and crustaceans occur. These in turn attract a wider variety of fish species than is seen on storm beaches. Worm beds will be evident from casts at the surface, while shellfish, crabs and prawns can all be collected from groynes and from around the supports of piers.

Reaching open beaches doesn't usually entail a long walk, which allows more gear to be taken. A standard setup would comprise a 12ft beachcaster to throw 4 to 6oz leads (wired where used in strong currents), coupled with a large fixed spool reel or multiplier capable of holding 250 yards of 20lb line. Multipliers fitted with level winds and magnetic braking systems ensure problem-free casting. A two- or three-hook flapper rig completes the setup.

During summer, expect to catch flounders, plaice, dabs and perhaps even sole using crab and worm baits. Mackerel will also often be close inshore chasing sprats, and can be caught on spinners or teams of feathers. After dark, target rays with sand eels and peeler crab.

FISH'N'TIPS

▶ *When distance casting always use a 60 lb shock leader between reel line and hooklength.*

BELOW Open beaches are more benign and richer environments than storm beaches; they slope more steeply, reducing the need for long-distance casting to reach deep water.

Boat Fishing
Charter Boat Fishing

Going afloat offers the chance of catching a variety of species, some probably for the first time, of a good size and in large numbers. Big pollack haunt reefs, ling and conger eels carpet wrecks, while rarer fish like skate, sharks and even giant bluefin tuna can be caught in British waters.

Summer sees migrant species appear and, when the weather is calm, it is the perfect time to try out charter boat fishing. If you are new to charter boat fishing, tag along with experienced boat anglers from a club or contact a skipper directly to book a place. Alternatively, organise your own group. It would be worth trying a "taster" half-day or evening trip first. Most charter boats are licensed to carry twelve anglers, though eight to ten is best as it minimises the time wasted untangling lines! Ask the skipper's advice on the marks that will be visited, the species likely to be encountered and the tactics and tackle required; use the checklist below when packing.

Charter boats offer life jackets and a full array of safety equipment. Many hire rods,

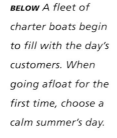

BELOW A fleet of charter boats begin to fill with the day's customers. When going afloat for the first time, choose a calm summer's day.

KIT CHECKLIST

Several layers of clothing
Waterproofs
Wellingtons
Lunch
Sun cream
Sunglasses
Hat
Camera
Seasickness medication
Boat rod and gear (optional)

LEFT Boat fishing offers the chance of catching big fish of many different species and often in large numbers.

FISH'N'TIPS

▶ Items lost overboard stay lost – wrist straps can save cameras!

reels and end tackle, but check beforehand as some may expect you to bring rods and gear with you. Equipment hire is often included in the charter fee.

Avoid hangovers and big cooked breakfasts, and eat your breakfast at sea. The sea's motion may cause seasickness, and afflicted anglers head for the stern because it moves the least, but it is exposed and the engine exhaust fumes make it worse. Motion sickness pills help some anglers.

Never leave rigs or hooks lying around, and stow rods upright. Standard boat rods rated at 30lb should be paired with multiplier reels holding braid or monofilament main line.

ABOVE Offshore it is rarely calm and is often cool, so take plenty of warm, windproof and waterproof clothing.

RIGHT An excellent brace of cod caught from a deep-water wreck on baited pirks. Good charter boats provide top-quality tackle as part of the day's fee.

BELOW A good flatfish is netted, but the likelihood of tangles is high with so many anglers aboard.

Monofilament is better for novices. Setting the reel's drag properly is vital if fish are not to be lost – ask the skipper to help. Reels hold more braid because of its thin profile, but under tension it can cut to the bone. Weaker monofilament leaders should be attached to braid main line, so that if they snag and you need to pull hard for a

break, it is the cheaper monofilament that fails.

Usually the first task of the day on summer trips will be to catch some mackerel for use as fresh bait. Use a string of feathers and lower them to the bottom. Then wind in a few turns to minimise snagging, and jig by raising and lowering the rod tip. Mackerel may hit

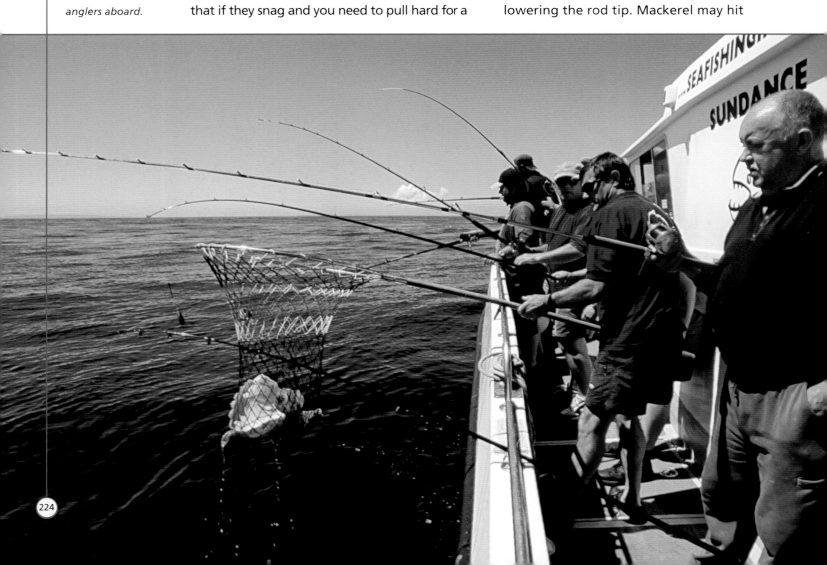

feathers in midwater on their way down, and this will be indicated by the line going slack. Once the bait box is full, the skipper will move on to the proper fishing marks!

Adding mackerel strip to the bottom feathers on a leader will attract wrasse, pollack, coalfish, scad and pouting on any reef mark. Small ling, codling, gurnard and a host of species are possible.

Ask the skipper's advice. To locate bigger fish, try a boom with a flowing trace that

ABOVE Some charter boats on the west coasts of Scotland (Mull) and Ireland (Westport) specialise in fishing for huge skate.

holds either a shad, a mackerel fillet or flapper – again, the skipper will be happy to show you how to do it. Thumb the spool to slow the rig's descent as this should stop it tangling. When a fish is hooked, keep the rod tip high to dampen the effect of its wild lunges, and let the reel's drag do the work. Allow the fish to

FISH'N'TIPS

▶ *Use sun protection often – on calm, dull days, that gentle breeze will "burn" you faster than the sun.*

RIGHT *Unhooking an unwanted conger eel. Good skippers will make themselves available throughout the day to bait hooks, sort out tangles and deal with any fish you've hooked.*

strip line against the drag, then wind in and retrieve line when you can. Be patient. Avoid swinging the lead and/or hooks aboard wildly as you land a fish. Gaff or net big fish; any you do not want should be released while still in the water. Merely handling some species will kill them, mackerel being a prime example.

Drift fishing needs a tidal flow, and around slack water, fish may well stop feeding for a time. Try jigging the bait or reel in alternately fast then slow up to midwater. If you feel a plucking on the line, speed up – a strong bite will often follow.

Two methods are practised from an anchored boat. In the method known as downtiding, the bait is carried away behind the boat by the current. To fish the bait closer to the boat, add more weight of lead. On foul and snaggy ground, try to fish straight down: fishing further away increases losses. Use weak bottom links or paperclips to leads, and lure savers on jigs and pirks. If chumming (ground-baiting off the boat or anchor) downtide, fish will track the scent trail back to the boat.

Uptiding involves casting the bait away from the boat. In shallow water, fish steer clear of an anchored boat, being put off by

the noise of the current against the anchor rope or chain. Cast against the tide using a grip lead. Bites are indicated by the line falling slack as fish break out the lead, causing the end rig to be carried downtide. Quickly wind in the slack until you feel the weight of the fish on the line, then strike. In downtiding most fish hook themselves.

Charter boat fishing is great fun, safe and productive!

ABOVE Every year, specimen tope are caught from charter boats fishing in big estuaries such as the Thames.

FISH'N'TIPS

▶ *The skipper is the expert, so seek his advice.*

LEFT Fishing at anchor, presenting baits downtide behind the boat. A scent trail created by groundbaiting will draw fish uptide towards the boat – and hookbaits.

Inshore Dinghy

Although dinghy anglers do not venture as far out to sea as charter boat skippers, going afloat in a small craft still opens up numerous fishing opportunities not available from the shore. With experience and the proper equipment, dinghies can also be taken out to more distant deep-water reefs and wreck marks. However, such forays are much more weather-dependent than they would be than in a charter boat.

Most dinghy owners started off by going out in a friend's boat, and gradually over time got more and more involved in the running of the boat, before finally buying their own. However, as well as picking up knowledge in this way, it is also worth taking lessons covering all aspects of boat handling and navigation at night school. Local tackle shops and boat chandlers will usually have details of such courses.

Standard dinghy tactics include uptiding, drifting and downtiding, but because of their manoeuvrability and shallow draught, dinghies can be used to drift close by and over offshore rocks and reefs in search of bass and pollack without grounding. Closer to the shore, a dinghy can be quietly and precisely worked along a rocky coastline with the aid of an electric motor, while plugs are fished along the edge for wary bass. Anchoring just off rocks and cliffs that drop away into deep water will produce battling pollack to lures and big ballan wrasse to legered hardback crab. The seabed here can

BELOW Netting a big lure-caught bass. Excellent sport can be enjoyed from dinghies, including well offshore over deeper wrecks and reefs when weather conditions permit.

▶ Unlike on charter boats, everyone in a dinghy should reel in to give the angler with a fish "on" the best chance of landing it.

▶ For two-stroke engines, mix the fuel/oil in the spare tank while ashore, not at sea!

▶ Always wear a life jacket when out on the sea. Automatically-inflating versions are much less cumbersome to wear.

BELOW A wide variety of flatfish will be present over inshore sandy shallows, including dabs (shown here), flounders and plaice.

ABOVE You can have a lot of pleasure fishing from a small boat. Beware of dangerous rocks, excessively rough water and do not stray too far without the proper equipment.

be very snaggy, and any big wrasse hooked will head straight for it, so use weak bottom links and things like stones and old bolts as weights. Trotting small sand eels down the tide in such places will often account for garfish and bass during high summer.

Fishing in shallower water, particularly over a sandy seabed, brings the possibility of rays, including big blonde rays, and monkfish. Many river estuaries and large sandy bays offer sheltered fishing for dinghies and often produce exceptional tope fishing. For all these species, tackle up with a 30lb class boat rod.

Flatfish will also be present, and great fun can be had fishing for them with a really light outfit. Fish with a freshwater carp or spinning rod or a 12lb class boat rod, coupled with 8 to 10lb line, and you will be surprised what a good scrap flounders and plaice can put up. Bait with lugworm, ragworm or fish strip and add spoons and beads to the hooklengths as added attractors.

Fly-fishing for Sea Fish

RIGHT When fly-
fishing from rock
marks, always wear a
life jacket and
non-slip footwear.

While many saltwater species can
be caught with the fly, bass are
unquestionably the most sought-after species
and can be targeted at many places around
southern Britain and Ireland.

Bass are to be found along rocky coastlines,
in estuaries and open beaches and often in
very shallow water in search of food. Flies that
imitate small fish and sand eels, prawns and
crabs will all be successful.

The half-light of early morning and evening
is generally most productive, though bass can
be caught during the day, particularly when a
breeze ruffles the surface.

Fly-fishing for pollack from platforms can
be fast and furious, and often the fly is taken

BELOW Where rock
marks fall away into
deep water, fly-fish
close in for pollack
using a sinking line.

LEFT Mackerel will grab at any flashy fly resembling a small fish, and show remarkable strength and speed when hooked.

successful, and any bright fly resembling a small fish will be taken avidly.

Mackerel are another species that can be taken on small gaudy flies. Any angler only used to hauling them in six at a time on a beachcaster or boat rod would be amazed at a mackerel's turn of speed and strength when hooked on a fly outfit.

Various species of fly lay their eggs in seaweed washed up on the shore, and the maggots that emerge can be present in vast numbers. Thick-lipped mullet will come right to the water's edge to gorge on these maggots as they are washed into the sea by the rising tide. Small imitation maggots, either tied with latex or bought from tackle shops (where they are sold for coarse fishing), will fool mullet feeding in this fashion.

Fly-fishing in saltwater is essentially a sport of the summer months. For most situations, a standard 10ft reservoir trout rod rated for a 7-weight line will suffice. In windy conditions it may be necessary to use one a little heavier. Shooting heads enable flies to be cast further and worked for longer and are useful when fish are not showing close in. When wading or fishing from rock marks, it pays to use a line tray for trouble-free casting.

just as it is about to be lifted off and recast. Be prepared for a pollack's crash dive for the bottom – and for any snags there – once they are hooked.

Pollack often lie close in along rocky shorelines, especially where the bottom drops away quickly, and it is usually more productive to cast parallel to the rocks rather than straight out. Sinking lines, their density dependent on the water's depth, are most

FISH'N'TIPS

▶ *Smaller bass (under 3lb) swim in shoals. Catch one and there are likely to be more around so recast as soon as possible.*

▶ *Feed mashed bread to mullet then fly-fish for them with a small piece of artificial flake.*

LEFT Fly-fishing for bass is most productive at dawn and dusk, using patterns imitating crabs, prawns, small fish and sand eels.

FISHING ABROAD
by John Wilson

Exotic sports fishing overseas is fast becoming big business for tour companies, and why not? In some cases, after less than a day's travelling you can be chasing bone fish across a shallow flat in the Bahamas, or hunting the mighty mahseer in the foothills of the Himalayas in northern India. It's all there to be explored and the ten exotic, inspirational locations that follow are just a fraction of what is now available to the angler willing to travel.

BELOW Five species of Pacific salmon can be caught from the prolific Fraser River system in Canada's British Columbia. This fly-caught, chunky "chum" salmon is common in the 12 to 20lb size range, and fights like mad.

Canada: the Fraser River System, British Columbia

BELOW *An English angler experiences the awesome power of a Fraser River sturgeon as it crashes out close to the boat.*

At over 1000 miles in length and with an annual salmon run of over 50 million fish, comprising no less than five separate species of Pacific salmon, the Fraser is the world's greatest, un-dammed salmon-producing river. But still more incredible, as if so many salmon were not enough, the system also has the most prolific stocks of giant white sturgeon in the whole of North America. The sturgeon feed upon salmon eggs and on the adult carcasses (all five species of salmon die after spawning), and provide truly spectacular sports fishing. The giant white

sturgeon occasionally reaches phenomenal weights in excess of 1000lb, and is common in the 100 to 200lb size bracket, with fish of 300 to 400lb considered "weekly" catches. Small wonder that anglers from all over the globe travel to British Columbia.

A long-haul flight to Vancouver followed by a 70-mile road transfer going due east into the foothills of the Rocky Mountains, and you arrive at your final destination in the town of Chilliwack, or at Harrison Springs, the centres for coming to grips with both species. This is due to the phenomenal numbers of salmon

and sturgeon to be found where the Fraser converges with the clear-flowing, glacial-fed water of the Harrison River, itself fed by 40-mile long Harrison Lake and the Lilluet River system. Vast shoals of salmon – pink, coho, sockeye, chum and chinook (the largest of the five species, and commonly caught here at weights between 40 and 60lb) – can all be clearly seen in the fast, incredibly clear water of the Harrison River, and taken on a variety of methods. On the fly, an 8- to 10-weight single-handed outfit with either a floating or, better still, a sink-tip line is more commonly used, although a 13–14 Spey outfit is also ideal. Salmon are also taken from both boat and bank on spoon, on jigs, on trotted spinners, and on salmon eggs trotted beneath a float. "Bottom bouncing", which consists of bumping a fly down river close to the bottom using a long leader rigged to a swivelled ball ledger, can be successful. Dropping anchor and flipping a deep-diving plug 30ft downstream (the rod is then held firmly in a rest) so the pulsating lure attracts large chums and chinooks on their way upriver can succeed well.

Sturgeon are caught by downstream ledgering from a boat. Most of the guides' boats along the Fraser system are 18 to 23ft jet boats which take up to three anglers plus the guide. These whisk you along at speeds up to 50 miles an hour to get quickly from one

spot to another. The favoured rods (all tackle is supplied by the guide) are one-piece, 8ft "sturgeon specials" coupled to multipliers holding 100 to 130lb test braid. The 3ft hooklength (above which runs a sliding 6 to 16oz lead) is also braid, and sports a strong 6/0 hook baited either with an egg ball (salmon eggs wrapped in nylon stocking material), a piece of lamprey, or even a 3 to 4 inch square of rotting salmon flesh. Although sturgeon are known for biting gently, when hooked they often catapult themselves completely clear of the surface. Whether 50lb or 500lb, what a sight, and what a fight!

ABOVE Giant white sturgeon of 200lb, like this beauty, are considered almost everyday catches from the Harrison and Fraser rivers.

BELOW Huge chinook salmon, like this 40lb specimen, provide long, arm-wrenching tussles on light tackle and diving plugs.

South Africa's East Coast

A long-haul flight to Johannesburg and then a one hour domestic flight to Richards Bay on the prolific east coast opens up a wealth of exciting beach and boat fishing, going north all the way to the Mozambique border, with St Lucia being an ideal base. Here, along white sandy beaches, ragged tooth, bull, and sand sharks in the 200 to 400lb range are common catches following powerful battles lasting between one and two hours. These swim alongside Africa's largest bass, the kob (which can top 100lb), plus bluefish, garrick, threadfin salmon, several species of huge stingrays, giant trevalley, jacks, blue emperors and ladyfish. The period from December until May is prime time to fish from the shore, with offerings like squid, live-baits and freshly killed dead fish scoring heavily. Fourteen-foot, one-piece carbon surf rods and multipliers loaded with 30 to 40lb test monofilament plus wire traces (for the sharks) are standard tackle combos provided by all local guides along these surf beaches.

Trolling and bottom fishing offshore from South African-style 18 to 21ft boats (launched from the beaches) is perhaps even more exciting, with high-jumping species such as marlin, sailfish and dorado (in season) added to those already mentioned. There are also several species of tuna, plus a colourful array of hard-battling reef fish such as grunters and cave bass. A big shark or guitarfish is a far from unlikely catch while presenting cut bait at anchor just up from a reef or over broken ground. For the trolling, 30 to 50lb class outfits are supplied, while 20 to 30lb tackle is used at anchor or when drift fishing out over deep-water reefs where huge sharks are regular sightings, particularly massive tiger sharks weighing anywhere from 400lb to over 1000lb.

BELOW Spectacularly coloured species such as the blue emperor abound in the seas off South Africa's east coast.

RIGHT *Trolling offshore produces marlin, sailfish, tuna, and the high-leaping, fast-running and outrageously coloured Dorado, shown here.*

MAIN PICTURE *A huge sand shark, hooked over a shallow reef one mile offshore from St Lucia, is brought to the boat for unhooking.*

Egypt and Lake Nasser

MAIN PICTURE *This is merely one tiny bay in massive Lake Nasser, where the boats tie up for the night. This is wilderness fishing at its most exciting and remote.*

Stretching some 300 miles from the Sudan all the way north to the high dam in Aswan, Lake Nasser is of course a former desert area flooded by deliberately diverting the great River Nile to create one of the world's largest man-made lakes. It contains all the weird and colourful species of the Nile, from electric catfish to one of the world's largest freshwater fish, the Nile perch, which have been caught from the lake up to 230lb, plus vundu and sementundu catfish (both of which can reach over 100lb) and tiger fish. There is also a wealth of wildlife, from crocodiles and monitor lizards to exotic birds.

After a long-haul flight to Aswan, each fishing safari on the lake is via 25ft trolling boats (with an accompanying supply boat per 6 to 8 anglers), and can start from the dam itself in Aswan, or (via road transfers) from Garf Hussein (halfway down the western, Egyptian end of the lake) or from Abu Simbel,

close to the Sudanese border. A short tour around the impressive temples, built by Rameses II to impose fear upon the Nubians, usually precedes a fishing trip. Within a short time of leaving, you are in an entirely different, very silent world, totally devoid of all modern sounds. Here you will sleep on the boat, which is moored at night, and eat tasty Egyptian food. The only other souls to be seen are a few local net fishermen, who are very friendly.

Fishing consists of trolling big lures (using an uptide rod-multiplier outfit with 30lb monofilament, or 50lb braid line), 30 to 50 yards behind the boat at around 2–3 knots. The Nile perch wait in ambush, often ridiculously close in. Alternatively, you can cast into deep waters towards obvious features, but when that first Nile perch grabs hold, it could be anything from 20lb to 200lb.

RIGHT Trolling deep-diving and floating diving plugs accounts for the majority of huge Nile perch, but shore fishing can also offer some surprises.

ABOVE This is what everyone visits Lake Nasser to catch – a 100lb-plus Nile perch.

Brazil: Rio Negro, Amazonias

A long-haul flight to Manaus and then a 200-mile internal flight to Barcellos takes you to the banks of the Rio Negro. The river is up to 12 miles wide in places and is lined by dense rainforest. It is just one of 1000 tributaries that feed into the mighty Amazon; only a one-hour speedboat ride away upriver is the River Negro Lodge, where you can find some of the most spectacular and unusual freshwater fishing on the planet. The river is indeed rather dark, from the tannin which comes from sunken hardwood trees, but there is a definite benefit from this in that mosquitoes cannot breed in such water. Over 2000 species of freshwater fish exist here, from poisonous stingrays to giant catfish, both in the river at depths of up to 50ft and in numerous off-river lakes and lagoons. These form when

floodwater levels drop (fishing is only possible from October through to March). Most common are the thick-set and colourful red-tail, which can weigh more than a ton, and the piraiba, which is said to reach weights in excess of 400lb. There are piranhas too, the largest averaging over 2lb, plus three species of unbelievably colourful bass, the largest of which, the peacock, grows to nearly 30lb. The other two, the paca and butterfly bass, are much smaller but exquisitely marked and coloured. All three provide breathtaking sport both on the fly ("clouser minnow" and "deceiver" patterns on a 9- to 10-weight floating line outfit work best) and on surface plugs. Those with propellers at both ends that make an audible "wood-chopping" sound definitely produce more hits. When a big

BELOW Stunningly coloured red-tail catfish are just one of five catfish species to grow in excess of 100lb in the Rio Negro. This 25-pounder was just a baby!

peacock bass hits like a sledgehammer, an unforgettable, arm-wrenching battle will follow.

Amongst daily wildlife sightings are the noisy macaw parrots that constantly fly across the river, plus giant terns and kingfishers, egrets, herons and plovers, and many more Caiman crocodiles than are actually visible. There are freshwater porpoises too, in both grey and pink varieties. There is always a chance of seeing the inquisitive giant river otter as well.

To encounter the large catfish you need at least an 80lb test outfit, consisting of a powerful rod and a large-capacity multiplier for pumping these huge fish from their hideouts. There are no less than five species that grow to over 100lb, and due to the fallen hardwood trees littering the river bed close into the margins, only such a powerful rod will give you any chance of ever seeing one in a boat. Top baits are chunks of meat or chicken or a chunk of fish legered on the bottom. Short plugging rods coupled to small multipliers and braided line come as standard issue from your boat guide.

ABOVE The exquisitely coloured peacock bass fights like a demon on surface plugs and grows to nearly 30lb.

LEFT Averaging much less in weight than the peacock – the "paca" bass.

BELOW It is easy to understand why some say the butterfly bass is the prettiest of all.

Zambia and the Mighty Zambezi River

BELOW High-jumping, tooth-laden tiger fish like this chunky 16-pounder are common over double figures in the lower reaches of the Zambezi River.

This is Africa's fourth-longest river and the most easily accessible as far as exciting sports fishing is concerned. After passing over magnificent Victoria Falls (truly one of the world's wonders), it becomes the massive dammed 170-mile long Lake Kariba, then continues on its easterly course towards the second dam at Cahora Bassa. It is in these beautiful and wide lower reaches above Cahora Bassa – bordered on both sides by game-rich national parks (the northern bank being Zambia and the southern Zimbabwe) where commercial fishing is not allowed – that the very best sports fishing awaits visiting anglers, September and October being the prime time. A long-haul flight to the capital, Lusaka, is followed by a short domestic flight over forests of hardwood trees in a light aircraft.

ABOVE Elephants often come ridiculously close to the boat when you are fishing.

RIGHT Vundu, Africa's largest catfish, provide thrilling encounters from smelly legered offerings. Luncheon meat and soap (yes, soap) are among the top baits.

A short road transfer takes you to your fishing camp beside the river, where elephants, huge crocodiles, hippos, fish eagles, kites and carmine bee eaters are just some of the numerous daily sightings. Drift fish using strips of cut fish for the fearsome tiger fish, or anchor up in a quiet, deep spot and leger luncheon meat or a dead fish for Africa's largest and hardest fighting catfish, the "vundu". These can reach over 100lb, but are commonly taken in the 30 to 60lb bracket, and demand an uptide rod-multiplier outfit and 30lb line. The high-jumping tiger fish can be both enjoyed and subdued using a carp or heavy spinning rod and multiplier fixed-spool combo. A braided reel line of around 30lb test weight is recommended, and, due to this fish's awesome dentistry of 10 razor-sharp canines in its upper jaw, interlocking with eight in the lower, a 30lb-test, soft wire trace (plus 6/0 hook) is imperative, to say the least!

Canada: Wolf Lake, the Yukon

MAIN PICTURE *Playing 20lb-plus lake trout on the fly rod is more than a possibility in the Yukon. From the deep waters of Wolf Lake, fish of anything up to 60lb is possible.*

To reach this remote angling haven at Wolf Lake, a long-haul flight to the Yukon's capital, Whitehorse, is followed by an hour's float plane trip. A totally remote and pristine area of enchanting cold water, measuring some 13 miles by 3 miles, and surrounded by dense pine forests, it is in fact only reachable by float plane. Here, where bald eagles, osprey, moose and maybe a beaver or two are

daily sightings, monstrous great lake trout to over 60lb live, as well as exquisitely coloured and hard-fighting grayling in the crystal-clear and fast-flowing Wolf River, which exits from the lake. In the numerous shallow bays and inlets live unbelievably aggressive pike that are catchable on both lures and fly. Just like the lake trout, they need to be caught during the summer months to breed and feed up again in time for winter. "Ice out" in Canada's far north doesn't happen until May or even June, for instance. And it's "ice in" again

during October and November, when the whole cycle repeats itself; a harsh existence indeed. But, to the adventurous, travelling angler, it's a unique experience. July until September is prime fishing time here.

Only 8–10 anglers can stay here at any one time, so overcrowding is never a problem. In fact, you usually fish all day long without seeing another soul until you return to the lodge in the evening. Except for fly-fishing for grayling in the river (they average between 1 and 2lb here and battle like demons in the fast currents), which is best executed by wading and using a 5-weight, floating line outfit, fishing is from sturdy 16ft boats sporting 10-horsepower engines. The giant lake trout respond to both fly trolling and trolling big spoons. A Hi-D sinking fly line is imperative for keeping a large 3- to 5-inch fry pattern down deep enough on the troll (a 9–10 weight outfit being ideal), and a 9ft spinning rod coupled to a small multiplier loaded with 30lb braid is perfect for trolling.

INSET LEFT A 30lb-plus lake trout.

INSET RIGHT This small lake trout weighs just over 2lb.

North Norway Troms Region: Sea Fishing in the Fjords

Flights to Oslo and on to Tromso (actually above the Arctic Circle) put visiting sea anglers who are bent on having their string well and truly pulled by giant cod, specimen-sized halibut, haddock, coalfish and the strange wolf fish exactly where they need to be – amongst the cold, unbelievably clear and fertile waters of the Norwegian Fjords. Ideal bases, where boats and skippers are geared up for big fish, are at Skjervoy and on the island of Arnoy, also known as "Eagle Island". Incidentally, in addition to the awesome fishing, orcas, sperm whales, minke whales, springer whales and a number of porpoise species can be seen during most of the year.

Anglers primarily come here from far and wide to do battle with the largest cod in the world. Those that leave the Barents Sea spawn amongst the fjords during March and April, when monsters of 60lb-plus are on the cards. Cod over 100lb are taken commercially. It is therefore no secret that 20 to 30lb fish are taken daily, and there is always a chance of a 40- or 50-pounder, even during the summer months from June through to September. That truly magical period of around ten weeks' duration called "the midnight sun",

MAIN PICTURE AND INSETS *Hard-fighting coalfish (left) and cod (right) over 30lb from deep, crystal-clear waters, plus clear air, wholesome food and stunning scenery – these are the reasons why sea anglers visit Norway's fjords.*

when the sun never sets and when it is light enough even at 2 am to take a photo without a flash, is from mid-June to the end of August.

The cod here respond best to large pirks worked close to the bottom over rough ground. In order that you do not hook immature fish (which all too easily can get a 6/0 treble fully into their mouths),

pirks in the 6 to 16oz range are best fitted with 12/0 trebles. These take you straight through the "small-fish" barrier to those monster catches. Mind you, there is nothing to stop you from catching haddock, wolf fish and coalfish over 10lb, plus a halibut of anything over 100lb, while trying to catch big cod. North Norway's fjords are like that!

Spain: the River Ebro System

A flight into Barcelona, followed by a 130-mile road transfer to the sleepy town of Mequinenza, where the River Segre converges with the mighty River Ebro just below the high dam, brings you to the most prolific area, possibly in the whole of Europe, for both common carp and Wels catfish.

Fishing is from both boat and bank and accommodation can be found close to the river – tackle and bait are usually supplied by your guide.

The carp are hard-fighting common carp, which average on the large size (every other fish could be over 25lb, and specimens in the

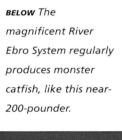

BELOW The magnificent River Ebro System regularly produces monster catfish, like this near-200-pounder.

LEFT Beautifully proportioned common carp are prolific; they average an exceptionally large size of between 20 and 35lb.

30 to 40lb range are weekly catches). This is due to the catfish feeding heavily on smaller carp and on the indigenous stocks of roach, tench and barbel. The best tactic is bolt-rig legering (a 3oz in-line lead and size 6–4 hook with an inch-long hair rig is ideal) over a swim prebaited with a multi-particle mix which includes hookbait samples such as 20mm boilies, maize, or 20 to 25mm halibut pellets.

In recent years, heavy baiting with halibut pellets has not only fed the carp but increased the weight of the catfish, to the extent that every other catfish is likely to top 100lb, with monsters of between 160 and 220lb around in very catchable numbers. Albino catfish in both yellow and white coloration, flecked in either green or black, are not uncommon in this part of the Ebro and Segre. Two or three 25mm halibut pellets, legered on a hair rig and strong 4/0 hook, in a swim that has been prebaited, is by far the most successful method for these catfish. Alternatively, legered squid or fresh fish baits

LEFT The wide reaches of the River Segre, where it merges with the Ebro in the town of Mequinenza, produces numbers of huge catfish.

(alive or dead) also bring success. To stand any chance of landing these monsters, you certainly need the powerful rods and large-capacity multipliers, loaded with 100lb test braid, as supplied by the guides. It is then a case of "hanging on".

USA: Arkansas Lakes and Rivers

MAIN PICTURE Lake Hamilton is renowned for the size of grass carp it holds. Specimens in the 25 to 50lb range await travelling anglers.

After flying into Little Rock, the capital of Arkansas, the choice of both lake and river fishing is quite staggering. And much of it is free once you have purchased a licence. There are over 50 species of freshwater fish, from cutthroat trout to huge alligator garfish topping 200lb, with no less than seven different species of carp, all of which can be over 40lb. These consist of three indigenous and three Asiatic species which have been introduced to control summer weed growth, plus common carp. The most widespread of these is the grass carp, which average on the large size (the state record being a staggering 80lb) and which fight incredibly hard, taking both surface and bottom baits. The best time to catch them is from May through to October.

The huge Lake Hamilton contains good stocks of grass carp, particularly in many of the shallow bays and off-lake inlets, where they can be taken on bolt-rig leger tactics (four grains of maize on a hair and size 4 hook, to 15lb test monofilament) over a prebaited area. To prepare maize, simply tip a sack of hard maize into a large cooler box and add several bags of sugar. Cover with boiling water, and stir. After several days, "fermentation" will take place, and though still hard, most carp species, particularly common and grass carp, just love its unique aroma. It will attract grass carp everywhere, whether you are legering or using simple float tackle. Grass carp are also attracted to bread and small mixer-type cat and dog biscuits, used in conjunction with a floating controller rig.

Another huge "oxbow lake" worth considering, measuring over 20 miles long by half a mile wide, is Lake Chicot, once part of the mighty Mississippi River. It averages around 12 to 15ft through the middle, and contains a strong population of both common and grass carp.

BELEOW (LEFT AND RIGHT) On relatively light tackle, grass carp to over 30lb provide unbelievably powerful scraps when summer water temperatures top 80 degrees.

Thailand: Commercial Freshwater Lakes with Giant Fish

A long-haul flight to Bangkok puts you within close reach of its most prolific, day-ticket, commercial fishery. This is called Bung Sam Ran, and it is in the suburbs north east of Bangkok, the capital of this truly fascinating country. An old clay pit of around 40 acres with depths to 20ft, the centre is one mass of rolling fish, many of them monsters. In addition to indigenous species like Chao Phray catfish over 100lb, Mekong catfish in the 40 to 200lb range, and giant Siamese carp to over 200lb, have been caught here (the lake holds numerous world records); fishery owners also stock with exotic South American species. So, visitors to Bung Sam Ran also have the opportunity of hooking into arapaima to 300lb, plus alligator garfish, pacu, red tail

BELOW 50lb-plus Mekong catfish are everyday catches from many of Thailand's commercial, day-ticket fisheries. There is no better bait than bread.

catfish, and many others. There are over 50 species in all, which makes up for all the associated clatter and noise of hundreds of anglers fishing! Heavy up-tide-style rods and multiplier outfits loaded with 50lb braid are advisable here, as you never know what's coming along next.

All these species can incidentally be caught using bread in various forms, either legered or float fished, and there are experienced local guides for hire who provide all the tackle and bait.

A worthwhile stop on your first trip is the two-lake, day-ticket Cha-am fish park, 130 miles south of Bangkok, close to the city of Hua Hin. This is another well-stocked commercial fishery, and there are many

ABOVE In addition to colourful indigenous freshwater species, South American monsters such as the arapaima, like this 100lb-plus beauty, are also caught.

LEFT Another South American species regularly taken over 20lb is the deep-bodied, hard-fighting pacu.

others, all fishable on a day ticket, scattered over the country. Cha-am is renowned for its strong head of swai and Mekong catfish, plus snake heads, giant Siamese carp and Chao Phray catfish. Again, bread is the best bait, and local guides with tackle are for hire. Waterside bungalows for overnight fishing are available at both Bung Sam Ran and Cha-am.

INDEX

ACKNOWLEDGEMENTS

Thanks go to the following people and organisations for their contribution to this book:

Total Angling *Shrewsbury, England* . . . . **www.totalangling.co.uk**
Newport Tackle *Newport, Shropshire, England* Special thanks to Joan Ashcroft,
Dave Lewis (sea fishing photography), *Cwmbran, South Wales*
Shakespeare Company (UK) Ltd., *England* . . . . **www.shakespeare-fishing.co.uk**
Loynton Fishing Tackle, *Staffordshire, England*
Simon Clarke – Catfish-Pro Ltd., *Farnham, England* **www.catfish-pro.com**

Fishing Abroad – Useful Contacts

Canada: Fraser River System, British Columbia . . . . **www.bcsportfishinggroup.com**
South Africa's East Coast . . . .**www.raggietackle.co.za**
Egypt and Lake Nasser . . . .**www.african-angler.co.uk**
Brazil: Rio Negro, Amazonias . . . .**www.peacockbassfishing.com**
Zambia and the Mighty Zambezi River . . . .**www.tailormadeholidays.co.uk**
Canada: Wolf Lake, the Yukon . . . .**www.yukon-adventures.co.uk**
North Norway Troms Region: the Fjords . . . .**www.troms-explorer.com**
Spain: the River Ebro System . . . .**www.garyallensregencyangling.com**
USA: Arkansas Lakes and Rivers . . . .**www.agfc.com**
Thailand: Commercial Freshwater Lakes . . . .**email: fishasia@ksc.th.com**

Conversion Chart

WEIGHTS and MEASURES

Inches	Cm	Mm
1	.2.54	.25.4
2	.5.08	.50.8
3	.7.62	.76.2
4	.10.16	.101.6
5	.12.7	.127
6	.15.24	.152.4
7	.17.78	.177.8
8	.20.32	.203.2
9	.22.86	.228.6
10	.25.4	.254
11	.27.94	.279.4
12	.30.48	.304.8

Feet	Metres
1	.0.304
2	.0.609
3	.0.914
4	.1.219
5	.1.524
6	.1.828
7	.2.133
8	.2.438
9	.2.743
10	.3.048

Yards	Metres
1	.0.914
2	.1.828
3	.2.743
4	.3.657
5	.4.572
6	.5.486
7	.6.4
8	.7.315
9	.8.229
10	.9.144

Oz	Grams
1	.28.34
2	.56.69
3	.85.04
4	.113.3
5	.141.7
6	.170
7	.198.4
8	.226.7
9	.255.1
10	.283.4

lb	kg
1	.0.453
2	.0.907
3	.1.36
4	.1.814
5	.2.267
6	.2.721
7	.3.175
8	.3.628
9	.4.082
10	.4.535

Drams	Grams
1	.1.771
5	.8.859
10	.17.718